D1590159

JANE AUSTEN

AND

SAMUEL JOHNSON

Peter L. De Rose

University Press
of America™

Copyright © 1980 by
Peter L. DeRose
University Press of America, Inc.™
P.O. Box 19101, Washington, D.C. 20036

Printed in the United States of America

ISBN: 0-8191-1074-4 (Perfect)
0-8191-1073-6 (Cloth)

Library of Congress Catalog Card Number: 80-7813

FOR MY MOTHER AND FATHER

CONTENTS

Preface   vii

Abbreviations   ix

I.   Jane Austen and Samuel Johnson   1

II.   Imagination in Northanger Abbey   15

III. Hardship, Recollection, and
      Discipline: Three Lessons
      in Mansfield Park   37

IV.   Marriage and Self-Knowledge in
      Emma and Pride and Prejudice   65

V.   Exploration of Feeling in Sense
      and Sensibility and Persuasion   93

      Epilogue   115

      Index   119

v

PREFACE

This study places Jane Austen in a specific ethical tradition, that of the eighteenth-century literary moralist, exemplified by Dr. Samuel Johnson, whose influence on her is demonstrable. It attempts, moreover, to resolve several issues which a twentieth-century critical sensibility raises about her novels: the meaning of "imagination" in Northanger Abbey, characterization in Mansfield Park, the appropriateness of marriage in Emma and Pride and Prejudice, and the relation of Persuasion to the earlier novels, especially Sense and Sensibility. Invariably these issues derive from an alleged contradiction between the art and the traditional morality of Jane Austen's fiction. By illuminating the Johnsonian norms which inform her six novels--developed extensively in Rasselas, in the Rambler, Idler, and Adventurer essays, as well as in Boswell's Life of Johnson-- and by demonstrating their aesthetic assimilation in the illustration of character, the determination of incident, and the exploration of theme, this study affirms the unity of Jane Austen's moral and artistic impulse. Johnsonian concepts, like the importance of self-knowledge and the repudiation of pride, of practical common sense in the face of real and imaginary deception, of rational self-control in the service of moral duty, and of recollection, discipline, and sacrifice in the difficult education for life, are aesthetically integrated in Jane Austen's fiction.

Earlier versions or portions of the following chapters have appeared in Studies in the Novel (Fall 1977), Renascence (Summer 1978), Notes and Queries (June 1979), and Publications of the Arkansas Philological Association (Summer 1977). I am grateful to the editors of these journals for permission to reprint my essays here.

I am happily indebted to Professors Paul N. Zietlow, Mary A. Burgan, Philip B. Daghlian, and Robert E. Gross, all of Indiana University, for

their careful and fruitful reading of these
chapters in the early stages of their preparation.
I am also grateful to my colleagues at Lamar
University, Professors Arney L. Strickland, Robert
C. Olson, Sterling W. McGuire, and Vernice M.
Monroe, who have provided me fellowship, encouragement, and support. I am pleased to acknowledge,
too, my gratitude to Mrs. Priscilla Burrows, for
her cheerful and expert typing of the manuscript.
Any errors of judgment or of fact, however, I
gracefully acknowledge as entirely my own.

P. L. D.

Lamar University
Beaumont, Texas
22 February 1980

ABBREVIATIONS

Jane Austen

E   Emma. The Novels of Jane Austen, ed. R. W. Chapman, 3rd ed. (1933; rpt. London: Oxford University Press, 1969), IV.

Letters   Jane Austen's Letters to Her Sister Cassandra and Others, ed. R. W. Chapman, 2nd ed. (1952; rpt. London: Oxford University Press, 1964).

MP   Mansfield Park. The Novels of Jane Austen, III.

MW   Minor Works. The Works of Jane Austen, ed. R. W. Chapman (1954; rpt. London: Oxford University Press, 1969), VI.

NA   Northanger Abbey. The Novels of Jane Austen, V.

P   Persuasion. The Novels of Jane Austen, V.

PP   Pride and Prejudice. The Novels of Jane Austen, II.

SS   Sense and Sensibility. The Novels of Jane Austen, I.

Samuel Johnson

Dictionary   A Dictionary of the English Language, 2 vols. (London, 1755).

Life   James Boswell, The Life of Samuel Johnson, ed. George Birkbeck Hill, rev. and enl. by L. F. Powell, 6 vols. (Oxford: Clarendon Press, 1934-64).

Lives	The Lives of the English Poets, ed. George Birkbeck Hill, 3 vols. (Oxford: Clarendon Press, 1905).
R	Rasselas, ed. R. W. Chapman (Oxford: Clarendon Press, 1927).
Works	The Yale Edition of the Works of Samuel Johnson, ed. Allen T. Hazen and John H. Middendorf (New Haven: Yale University Press, 1958--); eleven volumes now in print, 1980.

Full bibliographical information for other works consulted is provided in the footnotes.

A student may easily exhaust his life in comparing
divines and moralists, without any practical regard
to morality or religion; he may be learning not to
live, but to reason; he may regard only the elegance
of stile, justness of argument, and accuracy of
method; and may enable himself to criticise with
judgment, and dispute with subtilty, while the chief
use of his volumes is unthought of, his mind is
unaffected, and his life is unreformed.

Samuel Johnson, Rambler no. 87

       When the evening was over, Anne could not but
be amused at the idea of her coming to Lyme, to
preach patience and resignation to a young man whom
she had never seen before; nor could she help
fearing, on more serious reflection, that, like
many other great moralists and preachers, she had
been eloquent on a point in which her own conduct
would ill bear examination.

Jane Austen, Persuasion

CHAPTER I

JANE AUSTEN AND SAMUEL JOHNSON

A persistent problem in the criticism of Jane
Austen, which Marvin Mudrick perhaps best articu-
lates, is the alleged conflict between the author's
art and her morality. "Within the novels," Mudrick
asserts, "the conflict was between her subject,
with its frequent chunks of morality, and her ironic
genius, which could treat morality, if at all, only
most obliquely."[1] I do not wish to quarrel here
with Mudrick's insights--and he offers many--on
Jane Austen's ironic genius, but I do wish to take
issue with his argument that morality is unassim-
ilated in her novels. After the Jamesian fashion,
Mudrick grants the artist her subject, and attempts
to criticize only what she makes of it, and particularly

> that part of her subject containing im-
> personal and fossilized bits of eigh-
> teenth-century theological casuistry.
> These bits remain just bits, discrete
> fragments of something else which stick
> out of the otherwise organic texture of
> her novels: untransformed material, in
> short, which (to adopt another of James's
> celebrated dicta) neither determines in-
> cident nor illustrates character. Mor-
> ality is, of course, a possible subject,
> like any other interest of mankind; but
> it must be handled in terms of character
> and incident, not on its own terms.[2]

One way of coming to terms with this criticism is
to identify and illuminate the moral norms which
inform Jane Austen's fiction, and to demonstrate
the degree of artistic intensity with which they
are integrated in her work.

The moral norms, invariably expressed or implied in Jane Austen's novels, derive ultimately

1

from an orthodox, eighteenth-century English Christianity, and they affirm, in particular, the concepts comprehensively developed in the work of "the first moralist of the age," Dr. Samuel Johnson.[3] Traditional concepts--like the importance of self-knowledge and the repudiation of pride, of practical common sense in the face of real and imaginary deception, of rational self-control in the service of moral duty, and of discipline and sacrifice in the difficult education for life--traditional concepts like these are so pervasive in her fiction, in fact, that an awareness of the manner and extent to which they are assimilated, dramatized, and explored should make us realize that the conflict between Jane Austen's art and her morality is more apparent than real; and that, indeed, the pervasive and inflexible moral norms are the only sure means we have of measuring her ironic genius. Without them, for instance, we could never sympathetically understand a heroine like Fanny Price, whose values stand unmistakably--and ironically--at the center of Mansfield Park. Without them, we could never fully appreciate the irony by which Jane Austen undercuts Elizabeth Bennet when she is judging and acting wrongly. Morality in Jane Austen's fictional world is inseparable from her art. Examining the traditional, Johnsonian moral character of her novels, then, we shall discover another dimension of Jane Austen's artistic achievement.

Long before Mudrick's expression of the art-morality problem in Jane Austen's novels, A. C. Bradley recognized what he called the author's moralist and humorist strains, and accurately, if incompletely, related the first to Jane Austen's moralist predecessor of the eighteenth century, Samuel Johnson:

> These strains are often blended or even
> completely fused, but still they may be
> distinguished. It is the first that con-
> nects her with Johnson, by whom, I suspect,
> she was a good deal influenced. With an
> intellect much less massive, she still
> observes human nature with the same pen-
> etration and the same complete honesty.

2

She is like him in the abstention--no
doubt, in her case, much less deliber-
ate--from speculation, and in the orthodoxy and strength of her religion. She
is very like him in her contempt for mere
sentiment, and for that 'cant' of which
Boswell was recommended to clear his mind.
We remember Johnson in those passages
where she refuses to express a deeper
concern than she feels for misfortune or
grief, and with both there is an occasional
touch of brutality in the manner of the
refusal. It is a question, however, of
manner alone, and when she speaks her mind
fully and gravely she speaks for Johnson
too; as when she makes Emma say: 'I hope
it may be allowed that, if compassion has
produced exertion and relief to the suf-
ferers, it has done all that is truly
important. If we feel for the wretched
enough to do all we can for them, the
rest is empty sympathy, only distressing
to ourselves' (ch. 10). Finally, like
Johnson, she is, in the strict sense,
a moralist. Her morality, that is to say,
is not merely embodied in her plots, it
is often openly expressed. She followed
a fashion of the day in her abstract
titles, Sense and Sensibility, Pride and
Prejudice, Persuasion; but the fashion
coincides with the movement of her mind,
and she knew very well the main lesson
to be drawn from the other three novels.
Her explicit statements and comments are
often well worth pondering, though their
terminology is sometimes old-fashioned,
and though her novels contain infinitely
more wisdom than they formulate. [4]

Succeeding generations of Austen critics have
deepened our awareness of her affinities with
Samuel Johnson. In Mary Lascelles' seminal study,
for instance, Jane Austen is described as one who
"trained herself in Johnson's school." This training
appears in what Lascelles calls the author's "preg-
nant abstractions" (Lady Middleton and Mrs. Dashwood,

3

for example, "sympathized with each other in an
insipid propriety of demeanor, and a general want
of understanding" /SS, 229/); her "antithetic
phrasing" (Anne Elliot, advising Captain Benwick,
for example, "ventured to hope that he did not
always read only poetry; and to say, that she
thought it was the misfortune of poetry, to be seldom safely enjoyed by those who enjoyed it completely; and that the strong feelings which alone
could estimate it truly, were the very feelings
which ought to taste it but sparingly" /P, 100/);
and her "lively mimicry of idiom in oblique oration"
(Mrs. Phillips, for example, with her promise of
"a little bit of hot supper" /PP, 747; and Mr.
Shepherd, with his account of his chosen tenant--
"quite the gentleman" /P, 227).5   C. S. Lewis has
metaphorically described Jane Austen as the "daughter of Dr. Johnson," who "inherits his commonsense,
his morality, even much of his style." In her
novels, Lewis observes, "the great abstract nouns
of the classical English moralists are unblushingly
and uncompromisingly used; good sense, courage,
contentment, fortitude, 'some duty neglected, some
failing indulged,' impropriety, indelicacy, generous
candour, blameable distrust, just humiliation,
vanity, folly, ignorance, reason. These are the
concepts by which Jane Austen grasps the world.
In her we still breathe the air of the Rambler and
Idler." And all of Jane Austen's novels, Lewis
claims, embody strict moral values which are "those
of all the heroines, when they are most rational,
and of Jane Austen herself. This is the hard core
of her mind, the Johnsonian element, the iron in
the tonic."6 More recently, Frank Bradbrook im-
pressively suggests, "The fact that Jane Austen is
known to have been influenced by Dr. Johnson has
perhaps resulted in an underestimation of the range
and profundity of her indebtedness to him." He
adds, "The language of the two writers, the terminology that they use, is sometimes so close that
one can hardly distinguish one from the other."7
Curiously, however, the Johnsonian moral dimension
of Jane Austen's fiction has never been fully explored. While major critical studies have examined
in detail many of the formal aspects of her novels--

4

narrative technique, irony, structure, style--none
of them has focused completely on their traditional
moral character by defining the norms Jane Austen
inherits from the most influential literary moralist of her age, and by demonstrating the manner
in which these norms are woven into the organic
texture of her work.

There is ample biographical and textual jus-
tification for a study of this kind. Jane Austen's
extensive knowledge of and respect for Dr. Johnson's
work are affirmed in several sources--in the letters,
in the biographical studies, and, more importantly,
in the novels themselves. In a letter of 25
November 1798, addressed to her sister Cassandra,
for example, Jane Austen casually notes, "We have
got Boswell's 'Tour to the Hebrides,' and are to
have his 'Life of Johnson'" (Letters, 32-33). In
another letter (8 February 1807), there is a strong
indication that she did in fact read the Life rather
attentively. She opens with the expectation of
"having nothing to say" to Cassandra, yet she writes
several pages conveying news of a domestic nature,
and concludes with the ironic observation: "There,
I flatter myself I have constructed you a smartish
Letter, considering my want of Materials. But
like my dear Dr. Johnson I believe I have dealt
more in Notions than Facts" (Letters, 181). She
is apparently referring to Johnson's letter to
Boswell (4 July 1774), in which Johnson, having by
no means been attentive to minute accuracy in his
Journey to the Western Islands of Scotland, informs his correspondent: "I wish you could have
looked over my book before the printer, but it
could not easily be. I suspect some mistakes; but
as I deal, perhaps, more in notions than facts,
the matter is not great, and the second edition
will be mended, if any such there be" (Life, II,
279).

Among the biographers, Jane Austen's nephew,
James Edward Austen-Leigh, records in his Memoir
of Jane Austen that among his aunt's favorite
writers "Johnson in prose, Crabbe in verse, and
Cowper in both, stood high."[8] Henry Austen, who
wrote the Biographical Notice, prefixed to the

edition of Northanger Abbey and Persuasion, also
testifies that Johnson was one of her two "favourite
moral writers," Cowper the other (NA, 7). The degree of Jane Austen's preference for Johnson can
in some way be measured by the sympathetic manner
in which she refers to him in one of her few extant
poems, "To the Memory of Mrs. Lefroy"--written to
honor an intimate friend, who was killed by a fall
from her horse on Jane Austen's birthday (MW, 440-
42). Jane Austen alludes to Johnson in the last
two stanzas of the poem, and the quotation in the
penultimate stanza is adapted from Boswell's Life,
on 20 December 1784 (IV, 420-21):

> At Johnson's Death, by Hamilton, 'twas said,
> "Seek we a substitute--Ah! vain the plan.
> No second best remains to Johnson dead--
> None can remind us even of the Man."
>
> So we of thee--unequalled in thy race,
> Unequall'd thou, as he the first of Men.
> Vainly we search around thy vacant place,
> We ne'er may look upon the like again.
>   (MW.442)

Jane Austen's juvenile quatrains certainly have
few merits as poetry, but they do at least affirm
the deep impression occasioned by her friend's
death--and possibly the depth of the impression
made by her favorite literary moralist.

Samuel Johnson is one of the few writers to
whom Jane Austen explicitly and favorably alludes
in her Juvenilia and in her major novels. In
Northanger Abbey, for example, she obviously en-
dorses Henry Tilney's Johnsonian precision in the
use of language. As his sister Eleanor informs
the ingenuous Catherine Morland about her misuse
of language, "The word 'nicest,' as you used it,
did not suit him; and you had better change it as
soon as you can, or we shall be overpowered with
Johnson and Blair all the rest of the way" (NA,
108). In Mansfield Park, Edmund Bertram solici-
tously inquires about Fanny's reading: "How does
Lord Macartney go on?--(opening a volume on the
table and there taking up some others). And here

are Crabbe's Tales, and the Idler, at hand to relieve you, if you tire of your great book" (MP,
456). There is also Fanny's reflective comparison
of her two homes, which recalls a familiar passage
in Johnson's Rasselas: "In a review of the two
houses, as they appeared to her before the end of
a week, Fanny was tempted to apply to them Dr.
Johnson's celebrated judgment as to matrimony and
celibacy, and say, that though Mansfield Park might
have some pains, Portsmouth could have no pleasures"
(MP, 392).

Not only was Jane Austen obviously conversant
with Johnson's life and writings, but she also ev-
idently shared many of his intellectual, literary,
and moral tastes. The author of the Biographical
Notice observes, for instance, that Jane Austen
appreciated Samuel Richardson's power of creating
characters (particularly in Sir Charles Grandison),
though in her own art secure from his stylistic
prolixity and tediousness. Henry Austen adds that
she did not rank the work of Henry Fielding quite
so high. "Without the slightest affectation," he
writes, "she recoiled from every thing gross.
Neither nature, art, nor humour, could make her
amends for so very low a scale of morals" (NA, 7).
Having read Boswell's Life of Johnson, Jane Austen
would have been aware of Johnson's similar preference for Richardson over Fielding. "There is all
the difference in the world between characters of
nature and characters of manners," Johnson once
explained; "and there is the difference between
the characters of Fielding and those of Richardson"
(Life, II, 48-49). In other words, the difference
is "between a man who knew how a watch was made,
and a man who could tell the hour by looking on
the dial-plate." While it would seem that
Johnson's judgment hinges on fictional technique,
it is rather Fielding's moral shortcomings, as Ian
Watt cogently suggests, that were probably the de-
cisive factor in Johnson's disapproval.[9] Actually,
Johnson's repudiation of Fielding can be narrowed
still further to a strong dislike of Tom Jones and
of its harmful influence on innocent youth. Johnson
once told Hannah More that he "scarcely knew a more
corrupt work" than Tom Jones (Life, II, 174n). In

7

the Rambler no. 4, moreover, Johnson attacked the effects of "familiar histories" whose wicked heroes are made so attractive that "we lose abhorrence of their faults," apparently with works like Smollett's Roderick Random (1748) and Tom Jones (1749) chiefly in mind. One can safely surmise that Johnson considered Tom Jones a corrupting influence on youth not because of Tom's sexual escapades but because of Tom's notorious lack of principles. And with no moral principles to steady the conduct of this picaresque hero, Fielding advocates too strong a trust in the uncertain inclinations of the human heart.[10] With similar disapproval Jane Austen characterizes the unscrupulously deceptive and vulgar John Thorpe of Northanger Abbey as an unprincipled young cad, whose main interests are money, horses, and drinking and who has no time for reading novels--with the significant exceptions of The Monk and Tom Jones. Neither Johnson nor Jane Austen, it would seem, believed in the innate, or unprincipled, goodness of the human heart.

Further evidence indicates the strength of their common intellectual-moral interests. Both read widely in the moral literature of the age. Johnson, of course, also wrote numerous sermons and actively engaged throughout his life in religious-moral inquiry and dispute. He initiated the composition of the Rambler essays with a prayer (20 March 1750), which reveals the ardor that he brought to this work: "Almighty God, the giver of all good things, without whose help all Labour is ineffectual, and without whose grace all wisdom is folly, grant, I beseech Thee, that in this my undertaking thy Holy Spirit may not be withheld from me, but that I may promote thy glory, and the Salvation both of myself and others,--Grant this O Lord for the sake of Jesus Christ. Amen" (Works, I, 43). With identical fervor he concluded the final issue of this periodical:

> The essays professedly serious, if
> I have been able to evaluate my own in-
> tentions, will be found exactly conform-
> able to the precepts of Christianity,
> without any accommodation to the licen-

8

tiousness and levity of the present age.
I therefore look back on this part of
my work with pleasure, which no blame or
praise of man shall diminish or augment.
I shall never envy the honours which wit
and learning obtain in any other cause,
if I can be numbered among the writers
who have given ardour to virtue, and confidence to truth. (Rambler no. 208, V,
320)

By disposition and education Jane Austen's interests
took a similar turn. Notwithstanding what Laurence
Lerner calls the "solemn and splendid Pecksniffian
style" of Henry Austen's adulation, his conclusion
in the Biographical Notice well expresses the moral
seriousness with which Jane Austen endowed her life
and her work: "One trait only remains to be touched
on. It makes all others unimportant. She was
thoroughly religious and devout; fearful of giving
offense to God, and incapable of feeling it towards
any fellow creature. On serious subjects she was
well-instructed, both by reading and meditation,
and her opinions accorded strictly with those of
our Established Church" (NA, 8).[11] Jane Austen's
orthodoxy and moral inclination are understandable
enough. Her father, George, was a clergyman (the
Rector of Steventon in Hampshire) and two of her
brothers, James and Henry--as well as her nephew,
the author of the Memoir--were ordained clergymen.
The family library in Steventon, in which--for all
practical purposes--she received her education,
contained approximately five hundred volumes, a
good number of these presumably of a religious-
ethical nature.[12] One of Jane Austen's letters
(8 September 1816) indicates that she read her
cousin Edward Cooper's sermons, though she did not
like them, since they were "fuller of Regeneration
& Conversion than ever--with the addition of his
zeal in the cause of the Bible Society" (Letters,
467). In another of the letters (28 September
1814), Jane Austen observes, "I am very fond of
Sherlock's Sermons, prefer them to almost any"
(Letters, 406). Her preference of Sherlock suggests,
to R. W. Chapman at least, more than customary
religious observance, since Bishop Sherlock was

9

born in the seventeenth century and since his
sermons cannot have been ordinary reading of ladies
in the nineteenth.[13] Sherlock's Sermons were recommended with even greater respect by Dr. Johnson
on two occasions recorded in the Life (III, 248;
IV, 311). Jane Austen also implicitly recommends
the Scottish divine and professor of rhetoric,
Hugh Blair (1718-1800), when she has Mary Crawford
of Mansfield Park inquire about the efficacy of
preaching. "How can two sermons a week," Mary asks
Edmund, "even supposing them worth hearing, supposing the preacher to have the sense to prefer
Blair's to his own, do all you speak of?" (MP, 92).
Eleanor Tilney, in Northanger Abbey, too, refers
respectfully to the authority of Hugh Blair and of
Samuel Johnson. Jane Austen may have been aware
of Johnson's deep respect for Blair's work, which
Boswell represents on several occasions in the
Life. In one commendatory note to a publisher, for
example, Johnson writes, "I have read Dr. Blair's
first sermon with more than approbation; to say it
is good, is to say too little" (Life, III, 97).
Johnson warmly praised him at another time, when
in a lighter mood he claimed, "I love 'Blair's
Sermons.' Though the dog is a Scotchman, and a
Presbyterian, and every thing he should not be, I
was the first to praise them" (Life, IV, 98).

Recommended by abundant biographical and textual evidence, then, this study of the Johnsonian
moral character of Jane Austen's fiction illumi-
nates a dimension of her art which critics hitherto
have only partially explored. More importantly,
this study attempts to answer central critical
questions about the novels, which have arisen from
a failure to recognize the way Johnsonian morality
informs Jane Austen's art. By illuminating the
moral character of her fiction, the following chapters show how we may satisfactorily resolve such
critical issues as the meaning of "imagination"
in Northanger Abbey (Chapter Two), characterization in Mansfield Park (Chapter Three), the appropriateness of marriage in Emma and Pride and
Prejudice (Chapter Four), and the relation of
Persuasion to the earlier novels (Chapter Five).

10

Invariably, these issues have arisen from the projection of some modern assumptions onto a body of fiction which, though timeless, derives from an eighteenth-century moral ethos. By tracing the relationship between Jane Austen's work and that of a central literary moralist like Dr. Johnson, who undeniably exerted an influence on her, we shall discover intelligible answers to these perplexing questions.

Although some attempt has been made, in the arrangement of chapters, to preserve the chronology of Jane Austen's composition--Northanger Abbey, Mansfield Park, Emma, Persuasion--I have considered two of the novels, Sense and Sensibility and Pride and Prejudice, outside of their historical sequence. The critical issue isolated in each chapter may take precedence over Jane Austen's artistic development because of the consistency of her moral vision. I have assumed, too, that although Samuel Johnson is by no means a systematic moralist, his moral opinions are remarkably consistent throughout his career, and that they are expressed suitably both in his formal writing and in his informal conversation. Thus, while Jane Austen's moral heritage from Johnson is represented substantially in the works of his most important literary decade beginning in 1750--the Rambler, the Adventurer, the Dictionary, Rasselas, and the Idler--I have not hesitated, on pertinent occasions, to draw upon documentation either from Boswell's Life of Johnson or from Dr. Johnson's other works or obiter dicta.

NOTES

¹Marvin Mudrick, Jane Austen: Irony as Defense
and Discovery (1952; rpt. Berkeley: University of
California Press, 1968), pp. 221-22.

²Mudrick, p. 221n.

³Robert Voitle, Samuel Johnson the Moralist
(Cambridge, Mass.: Harvard Univ. Press, 1961), p.
vii, traces this epithet to the author of the
"History of the Science of Morals" which appeared
in the 1797 edition of the Encyclopaedia Britannica.

⁴A. C. Bradley, "Jane Austen: A Lecture,"
Essays and Studies by Members of the English
Association, 2 (1911), 14-15.

⁵Mary Lascelles, Jane Austen and Her Art
(1939; rpt. Oxford: University Press, 1968), pp.
107, 109, 110.

⁶C. S. Lewis, "A Note on Jane Austen," Essays
in Criticism, 4 (1954), rpt. in Ian Watt, ed., Jane
Austen: A Collection of Critical Essays (Englewood
Cliffs, N. J.: Prentice-Hall, 1963), pp. 23-24.

⁷Frank Bradbrook, Jane Austen and Her
Predecessors (Cambridge: University Press, 1966),
pp. 10, 16-17. Unfortunately, Bradbrook's demon-
stration of influence or affinity is sometimes
restricted to noting that Jane Austen says something that resembles a remark made somewhere by
Dr. Johnson.

⁸James Edward Austen-Leigh, Memoir of Jane
Austen, ed. R. W. Chapman (1926; rpt. Oxford:
Clarendon Press, 1967), p. 89.

⁹Ian Watt, The Rise of the Novel (1957; rpt.
Berkeley: University of California Press, 1971),
p. 280.

¹⁰See also Carey McIntosh, The Choice of Life:

12

Samuel Johnson and the World of Fiction (New
Haven: Yale University Press, 1973), p. 26.

[11]Laurence Lerner, The Truthtellers (London:
Chatto and Windus, 1967), p. 23.

[12]R. W. Chapman, Jane Austen: Facts and
Problems (1948; rpt. Oxford: Clarendon Press,
1950), p. 38.

[13]Chapman, Facts and Problems, p. 108.

CHAPTER II

IMAGINATION IN <u>NORTHANGER</u> <u>ABBEY</u>

Not only is <u>Northanger</u> <u>Abbey</u> a bold parody of
the Gothic-sentimental fiction popular in England
at the time of its composition, it is, as many
critics agree, a complex parody as well. In fact,
A. Walton Litz claims it would be a mistake to
read the novel as a "straightforward drama in
which . . . the disordered Imagination is put to
flight by Reason"; paraphrasing Lionel Trilling,
he asserts that "Catherine's belief in a violent
and uncertain life lurking beneath the surface of
English society is nearer the truth than the com-
placent conviction, shared by the readers of Mrs.
Radcliffe, that life in the Home Counties is always sane and orderly."[1] Andrew Wright similarly
concludes that "though we must reject the Gothic
world as inadequate and false, we cannot altogether
apprehend the real world by good sense alone.
Good sense, ironically, is limited too."[2] More
recently, Alistair Duckworth argues that while
<u>Northanger</u> <u>Abbey</u> undercuts Catherine's "imaginative
fantasy," the novel also dramatizes "the fallibil-
ity of the rational outlook."[3] Implicit in each
of these positions is the assumption that the
Gothic (or sentimental) and the real worlds are
not altogether different, and that together
Imagination and Reason will discover this. Such
an assumption, however, should not be made because
it misrepresents the Lockean epistemology which
underlies the literary burlesque in <u>Northanger</u>
<u>Abbey</u> and, equally significant, because it mis-
interprets Jane Austen's moral intention, shared
by writers like Samuel Johnson, to portray realistically the social dangers of everyday life.

To claim, as Wright does, that "there is more
on earth than mere common sense," or as Duckworth
claims, that Catherine's "imaginative responses"
lead to an "undefined recognition" of the truth,
or to suggest, as Litz and Trilling do, that
Catherine's imagination comes closer to the truth

than her reason, not only places the primary burden of knowing on the mental activity of reason or imagination, but also attributes to the imagination more truth-finding functions than Jane Austen and most other writers of her age would have believed possible.[4] It is truer to say that in the properly balanced mind, all mental activity--whether imaginative, rational, judgmental, or volitional--is secondary to the direct experience of sensory reality, and is, apart from experience, seriously suspect.[5] Applied to Northanger Abbey, this distinction leads to important conclusions about the parodic and realistic dimensions of the novel. First, Jane Austen's burlesque goes far beyond parody of mere literary form--whether Gothic or sentimental--to expose fully what Samuel Johnson calls in Rasselas the "dangerous prevalence of imagination" (R, xliii, 189). Second, by teaching heroine and reader alike to see things not as they are imagined but as they actually are, the comic-realistic episodes of Northanger Abbey serve a genuine moral purpose--to provide "the young, the ignorant, and the idle," as Dr. Johnson characterized the readers of popular fiction, with "lectures of conduct, and introductions into life" (Rambler 4, Works, III, 21).

I

To fully appreciate Jane Austen's burlesque of the imagination, we must recall the two philosophical premises on which John Locke's highly influential epistemology is built--that the mind at birth is a tabula rasa, which possesses no innate ideas, and that all our ideas (and all our knowledge) originate in inescapable human experience, either through sense-perception or reflection. "All those sublime thoughts which tower above the clouds, and reach as high as heaven itself, take their rise and footing here," Locke formulates in one of the most famous sentences in An Essay Concerning Human Understanding; "in all the great extent wherein the mind wanders, in those remote speculations it may seem to be elevated with, it stirs not one jot beyond those ideas which sense or reflection have offered for its contemplation."[6]

16

Since the mind, in all its rational thinking, can contemplate "no other immediate object but its own ideas" offered through sense-perception and reflection, all knowledge is "nothing but the perception of the connexion of and agreement, or disagreement and repugnancy of any of our ideas."[7]

Jane Austen may or may not have read Locke's Essay, but certainly she was familiar with Samuel Johnson's essays and with Boswell's Life of Johnson.[8] Heavily influenced by Locke's theory of cognition, Johnson's thought invariably reflects the philosophical importance Locke attached to the experiential basis of ideas and of knowledge. Johnson once told Boswell: "Human experience which is constantly contradicting theory, is the great test of truth" (Life, I, 454). And he is reported to have told George Staunton, who was about to travel to America for scientific purposes: "Trust as little as you can to report; examine all you can by your own senses"(Life, I 367). Johnson's dramatic refutation of Bishop Berkeley's idealism, in which he struck his foot "with a mighty force against a large stone till he rebounded from it," indicates how strongly he believed in the reality of a material world and therefore how close the ties are between human knowledge and objective, inescapable experience (Life, I, 471). Again and again, whether speaking casually or writing formally, he asserts that we do not know anything except what we have learned from direct or vicarious experience.[9] Even the poet is not in any contemporary sense "inspired," for "Where nothing has been put in the brain," Johnson says, "nothing can come out of it to any purpose of rational entertainment." Johnson certainly agrees with Imlac the poet, who claims that he can entertain himself because he has "a mind replete with images" culled from experience (R, xii, 62).

In acquiring knowledge, that is, in the process by which ideas and images are presented to the mind, and are arranged, classified, abstracted, and compared, the faculty of imagination (synonymous in the eighteenth century with "fancy") plays a necessary, if somewhat humble, function. Primarily a visualizing power, "imagination" is defined in Johnson's Dictionary as "Fancy; the power of forming ideal pictures; the power of representing things absent to one's self or others." Isaac Watts, whom Johnson draws upon for numerous illustrations in his Dictionary, defines the term in essentially the same way. "Our imagination," Watts says, "is nothing else but the various appearances of our sensible ideas in the brain, where the soul frequently works in uniting, disjoining, multiplying, magnifying, diminishing, and altering the several shapes, colours, sounds, motions, words, and things, that have communicated to us by the outward organs of sense. It is no wonder therefore," Watts cautions, "if fancy leads us into many mistakes, for it is but sense at second hand."[10] The problem of error lies in the fact that though the imagination can accurately represent images or ideas to the mind, it can also rearrange their parts in ways that do not correspond with the experienced nature of things. Hence, the distinction in Locke's terminology between "real" and "fantastical" ideas. "By real ideas," Locke explains, "I mean such as have a foundation in nature; such as have a conformity with the real being and existence of things, or with their archetypes. Fantastical or chimerical, I call such as have no foundation in nature, nor have any conformity with the reality of being to which they are tacitly referred, as to their archetypes."[11]

Dr. Johnson's vigorous distrust of the imagination derives, therefore, from the traditional belief that by so transforming real images or ideas this mental faculty entices man to escape reality (and to avoid action) by withdrawing into an illusory world--often of extreme beauty, horror, or adventure. Johnson's definition of "imagination," as well as its synonyms and cognates, amply demonstrates his profound misgivings toward this faculty. "Imagination" means not only the "power of forming ideal pictures," but also "Contrivance; scheme" and "An unsolid or fanciful opinion" (Dictionary). "Imaginary" means "Fancied; visionary; existing

18

only in the imagination." The primary meaning of
"Fancy" is "imagination," but it also signifies
"False notion" and "Something that pleases or
entertains without real use or value." The verb
"To fancy" means "To believe without being able to
prove." The cognate "fantastical" means "Irrational;
bred only in the imagination; Subsisting only in
the fancy; imaginary; Unreal; apparent only; having
the nature of phantoms; Capricious; humourous; un-
steady; irregular; Whimsical; fanciful; indulgent
of one's own imagination." Though the imagination
performs the necessary function of visualizing for
the mind, the liberality with which Johnson describes its powers in disapproving terms leaves no
doubt that he believed it to be a faculty considerably more capable of harm than good.

Johnson's distrust of the imagination is
doubtless based on the omnipresent possibility of
being deceived by this mental faculty. In Rambler
no. 125, Johnson refers to the imagination as a
"licentious and vagrant faculty, unsusceptible of
limitations, and impatient of restraint" (Works,
IV, 300). In Rambler no. 89, he draws the brief
portrait of the dreamer, who "retires to his
apartments, shuts out the cares and interruptions
of mankind, and abandons himself to his own fancy."
In his solitude "new worlds rise up before him,
one image is followed by another, and a long
succession of delights dances round him." When at
length he returns to society, the dreamer becomes
peevish "because he cannot model it to his own
will. . . . The infatuation strengthens by
degrees, and, like the poison of opiates, weakens
his powers, without any external symptom of malig-
nity" (Works, IV, 106). The dreamer later re-
emerges in Rasselas with a slightly fuller
characterization as the obsessed, paranoiac astronomer, who personifies "the dangerous prevalence of
imagination." The astronomer spends "days and
nights, in imaginary dominion, pouring, upon this
country and that, the showers of fertility, and
seconding every fall of rain with a due proportion
of sunshine" (R, xli, 185). But, as Imlac fright-
eningly explains to Rasselas:

19

There is no man whose imagination
does not sometimes predominate over his
reason, who can regulate his attention
wholly by his will, and whose ideas will
come and go at his command. No man will
be found in whose mind airy notions do
not sometimes tyrannize, and force him
to hope or fear beyond the limits of
sober probability. All power of fancy
over reason is a degree of insanity; but
while this power is such as we can con-
troul and repress, it is not visible to
others, nor considered as any depravation
of the mental faculties: it is not pro-
nounced madness but when it becomes un-
governable, and apparently influences
speech or action.

* * *

In time some particular train of
ideas fixes the attention; all other
intellectual gratifications are rejected,
the mind, in weariness or leisure, re-
curs constantly to the favourite conception, and feasts on the luscious
falsehood, whenever she is offended with
the bitterness of truth. By degrees, the
reign of fancy is confirmed; she grows
first imperious, and in time despotick.
Then fictions begin to operate as real-
ities, false opinions fasten upon the
mind, and life passes in dreams of rapture or of anguish. (R, xliii, 189-91)

In all her novels, Jane Austen consistently
dramatizes the imagination's "dreams of rapture"
and "luscious falsehood," which Imlac alarmingly
describes to Rasselas. When Elinor Dashwood, in
Sense and Sensibility, realistically refuses to
speculate about the fragments of Colonel Brandon's
mysterious narrative, for example, her sister
Marianne, we are told, would have speedily and
mistakenly fabricated an entire story "under her
active imagination" (SS, 57). In Pride and
Prejudice, the high-spirited Lydia Bennet, who

marries a charming rake, tends to see the world
through "the creative eye of fancy" (PP, 232).
Edmund Bertram, in Mansfield Park, for a long time
forms an illusory conception of Mary Crawford, who
he eventually tells Fanny has been "the creature
of /his/ own imagination" (MP, 458). Emma
Woodhouse, an extraordinary "imaginist" who can
take "an idea and make every thing bend to it,"
learns after many blunders the necessary "subjection
of the fancy to the understanding" (E, 335, 37).
Even Anne Elliot of Persuasion, the most rational
of all Jane Austen's heroines, embarrassingly
recognizes "What wild imaginations one forms, where
dear self is concerned!" (P, 201).

Catherine Morland, more than any other Austen
heroine, is particularly susceptible to the imagination's "luscious falsehood" and "dreams of
rapture." A few days after her introduction to
Henry Tilney, for example, she searches for him
all over the Upper and Lower Rooms of Bath, but
her inquiries are futile, for Henry has unex-
pectedly left the city, without even leaving his
name in the social register. "This sort of myste-
riousness, which is always so becoming in a hero,"
Jane Austen wryly comments, "threw a fresh grace
in Catherine's imagination around his person and
manners, and increased her anxiety to know more
of him" (NA, 35-36). Unable to learn anything of
Henry's absence from her friends, the Thorpes,
but encouraged by Isabella to think of him,
Catherine indulges her imagination on Henry's
character, and "his impression on her fancy was
not suffered to weaken." John and Isabella's plan
to ride to Blaize Castle is especially delightful
to Catherine's imagination, disappointed as she
has been by her interrupted engagement with the
Tilneys. "The delight of exploring an edifice
like Udolpho, as her fancy represented Blaize
Castle to be," Jane Austen explains, "was such a
counterpoise of good, as might console her for
almost anything" (NA, 86). General Tilney's invitation later to visit Northanger Abbey is even
more delightful in Catherine's imagination, for
her "passion for ancient edifices was next in
degree to her passion for Henry Tilney--and castles

and abbeys made usually the charm of those reveries
which his image did not fill" (NA, 141). Even
after Catherine is disabused of all her fancied
expectations about Northanger and the General,
she looks forward with still greater imaginary
delights to Henry's humble parsonage at Woodston:
"What a revolution in her ideas! she, who had so
longed to be in an abbey! Now, there was nothing
so charming to her imagination as the unpretending
comfort of a well-connected Parsonage, something
like Fullerton, but better" (NA, 212).

Although Catherine is particularly susceptible
to "dreams of rapture," no one in Northanger Abbey,
save perhaps Henry Tilney, really escapes the deceptions of an active fancy. When her social
climbing friend Isabella receives James's letter
announcing his parents' approval of their engagement, she (mistakenly) "knew enough to feel secure
of an honourable and speedy establishment, and her
imagination took a rapid flight over its attendant
felicities" (NA, 122). Even as reliable a figure
as Eleanor Tilney acknowledges her susceptibility
to the deceptions of the fancy. Though she recognizes, in one of her many conversations with
Catherine, that historians are as capable as literary writers of "flights of fancy" and of "imagination," she claims, "I am fond of history--and
am very well contented to take the false with the
true" (NA, 109). As for the imaginary "embellish-
ments" with which historians sometimes write,
Eleanor concludes simply: "They are embellish-
ments, and I like them as such. If a speech be
well drawn up, I read it with pleasure, by whom-
soever it may be made--and probably with much
greater, if the production of Mr. Hume or Mr.
Robertson, than if the genuine words of Caractacus,
Agricola, or Alfred the Great." But while Eleanor
knows that the historian's pleasurable "flights of
fancy" are not true, Catherine does not.

Thus far, Catherine's imagination has been
responsible for relatively harmless sallies of
unreality. It is capable of much worse. As Dr.
Johnson never tired of pointing out, "All power
of fancy over reason is a degree of insanity (R,

22

xliii, 189). A faithful representation of the
prevailing Lockean epistemology, the poet Imlac's
discourse to Rasselas on the ideas that despoti-
cally take hold of the mind recalls the passage
in Locke's chapter "Of the Association of Ideas,"
in which he observes: "I shall be pardoned for
calling /an unreasonable association of ideas/
by so harsh a name as madness, when it is considered that opposition to reason deserves that name,
and is really madness; and there is scarce a man
so free from it, but that if he should always, on
all occasions, argue or do as in some cases he
constantly does, would not be thought fitter for
Bedlam than civil conversation."[12] Some of our
ideas, in Locke's theory, have a "natural" corre-
spondence and connection, which reason discerns.
Other ideas, however, are connected wholly by
chance or custom, and have no reasonable corre-
spondence "founded in their peculiar beings."[13]
Yet they become so united in men's minds that it
is very hard to separate them. "The ideas of
goblins and sprites," Locke explains in a characteristic example, "have really no more to do
with darkness than light: yet let but a foolish
maid inculcate these often on the mind of a child,
and raise them there together, possibly he shall
never be able to separate them again so long as
he lives, but darkness shall ever afterwards bring
with it those frightful ideas, and they shall be
so joined, that he can no more bear the one than
the other."[14]

Jane Austen, it would be fair to say, considers Catherine Morland's chance association of
ideas in her imagination as a "degree of insanity."
In a significant conversational exchange with
Eleanor and Henry Tilney, for example, Jane Austen
comically anticipates the "madness" to which
Catherine's imagination eventually leads when the
young heroine informs her friends that "something
very shocking indeed, will soon come out in London,"
that she does not know "who is the author," that
it is to be "more horrible than any thing we have
met with yet," and that she "shall expect murder
and every thing of the kind" (NA, 112). Misin-
terpreting Catherine's rather obvious references

23

to the publication of a new Gothic novel, Eleanor
imagines instead a large-scale social riot. Henry
therefore steps in to clear the air, and amusingly
reminds his sister of the danger of mental im-
balance: "My dear Eleanor, the riot is only in
your own brain. The confusion there is scandal-
ous." Asserting that Eleanor has not rationally
conceived that "such words could relate only to
a circulating library," Henry mockingly describes
for the two young women Eleanor's imaginary
horrors--"a mob of three thousand men assembled
in St. George's Fields; the Bank attacked, the
Tower threatened, the streets of London flowing
with blood, a detachment of the 12th Light
Dragoons, (the hopes of the nation,) called up
from Northampton to quell the insurgents, and the
gallant Captain Frederick Tilney, in the moment of
charging at the head of his troop, knocked off his
horse by a brickbat from an upper window" (NA, 113).
Although Eleanor is the immediate object of Henry's
ridicule, the larger butt of irony here is the
naive imagination, which functions without commonsense attention, observation, and experience. To
credit Henry's rebuke of imaginary terrors with a
larger and "subversive" dramatic irony which ultimately vindicates the imagination, since his
description is constructed out of the actual de-
tails of the 1780 Gordon Riots and since the entire scene foreshadows the metamorphosis of
Catherine's imaginary horrors at Northanger Abbey
into the real social dangers of Bath--as several
critics have done--is to misread the pervasive,
fundamental irony that imagination, in operating
independently of real, factual experience, has
led the individual to a kind of intellectual
disorder, which Henry calls a "riot" in the
brain.15

     Surely the principal meaning that emerges
from Catherine's experiences at Northanger Abbey
is that her imagination--like Eleanor's in this
scene--has led to an aptly described mental
"riot," in which Gothic expectations are thoroughly entangled in her mind. Her 'premature ideas
about the abbey, for example, are a disturbing
collection of Gothic ramparts and cloisters,

"long damp passages," "narrow cells and ruined chapel," "traditional legends," and "some awful memorials of an injured and ill-fated nun." So active are Catherine's thoughts that even after her inquiries are matter-of-factly answered by Eleanor, Catherine is certain that Northanger Abbey conforms to her imaginary expectations. Good-naturedly teasing Catherine about these expectations on the drive to the abbey, Henry smiles and inquires if she has "formed a very favourable idea of the abbey" (NA, 157). "To be sure I have," she briskly replies, "Is not it a fine old place, just like what one reads about?" But a "fine old place" and "what one reads about" are hardly the same thing. Entering the grounds of the abbey along a "smooth, level road of fine gravel, without obstacle, alarm or solemnity of any kind" seems to her "odd and inconsistent" with her preconceived ideas (NA, 161). She does not expect to see furniture that displays all the "elegance of modern taste." The fireplace of her imagination, of "ample width and ponderous carving of former times," proves to be only a "Rumford, with slabs of plain though handsome marble, and ornaments over it of the prettiest English China." The Gothic windows, too, all "so large, so clear, so bright," are "yet less what her fancy had portrayed." In fact, "to an imagination which had hoped for the smallest divisions, and the heaviest stone-work, for painted glass, dirt and cobwebs, the difference was very distressing" (NA, 162).

But Catherine's habitual association of Gothic structures with the Gothic horrors she has read about is not easily disentangled. Her imagination eagerly presses forward to find something distressing in her situation. In her room she finds a large chest, which to Catherine's imagination is "strange indeed" (NA, 163). It does not occur to her that the remains of its silver handles have worn with age. On the contrary, her fancy suggests that they have been prematurely broken "by some strange violence." On the lid is clearly painted the letter "T," which she might reasonably assume represents "Tilney," but to Catherine's imagination it is a "mysterious cypher." She impatiently opens

the chest only to find a white cotton bedspread.
On her return to the room after dinner, the sight
of the old chest is an embarrassing reminder of
the "causeless fears of an idle fancy," yet the
sudden discovery of an antique black cabinet only
generates her fanciful associations once more.
The following morning's examination teaches her
the "absurdity of her recent fancies"--the correc-
tive to her imaginary ideas being the actual material evidence before her eyes (NA, 173).
Glancing over the page with a startled look,
Catherine wonders, "Could it be possible, or did
not her senses play her false?--An inventory of
linen, in coarse and modern characters, seemed
all that was before her! If the evidence of sight
might be trusted, she held a washing bill in her
hand" (NA, 172).

Though humbled by experience of this kind,
Catherine fabricates an even larger train of ideas
about General Tilney. On the flimsy basis of the
General's unwillingness to show her a part of the
abbey and of his refusal to join her and Eleanor
on his wife's favorite walk, Catherine is convinced that the General must have tortured and
murdered her, or at least permanently immured her.
Learning that the General was dissatisfied with
Mrs. Tilney's portrait and that it hangs in
Eleanor's bedroom, instead of the drawing room
for which it was intended, Catherine most un-
reasonably surmises, "Here was another proof. A
portrait--very like--of a departed wife, not
valued by the husband!--He must have been dreadfully cruel to her!" (NA, 181). When the General
calls her hastily from one end of the house, his
"evident desire of preventing such an examination"
is an additional piece of evidence in her mind.
"Something," she speciously concludes, "was certainly to be concealed; her fancy, though it had
trespassed lately once or twice, could not mis-
lead her here" (NA, 186). As though in mockery
of the reasonable exertion of a balanced mind,
Catherine imagines "in all probability" that the
General has never entered his wife's room since
his dreadful torture of her. Horrible ideas
naturally spring into Catherine's mind, and she

finds "many examples to justify even the blackest
suspicions" (NA, 187). At length Catherine de-
cides to explore the rooms and find material proof
to satisfy her suspicions, but all she discovers
is a "large, well-proportioned apartment, an handsome dimity bed, arranged as unoccupied with an
housemaid's care, a bright Bath stove, mahogany
wardrobes, and neatly-painted chairs, on which
the warm beams of a western sun gaily poured
through two sash windows"--metaphorically shedding
on Catherine's mind "a ray of common sense" (NA,
193). Henry Tilney's pointed reminder to her,
when he discovers her in the empty room, emphasizes
the significant aspect of her cognitive awakening.
"What have you been judging from?" he asks,
"consult your own understanding, your own sense
of the probable, your own observation of what is
passing around you. . . . Dearest Miss Morland,
what ideas have you been admitting?" (NA, 197-98).
Judgment, understanding, observation, a sense of
the probable--all play a significant role in
Catherine's release from the associations of her
imagination. The "visions of romance," we are
told, are now over. Completely awakened,
Catherine's eyes have been opened to the "extrav-
agance of her late fancies" and to the "liberty
which her imagination had dared to take." That
evening, before she retires, she clearheadedly
reflects on the foolishness which "had been all
a voluntary, self-created delusion, each trifling
circumstance receiving importance from an imagination resolved on alarm, and every thing forced
to bend to one purpose by a mind which, before
she entered the Abbey, had been craving to be
frightened" (NA, 200). Far from being a source
of truth, Catherine's imagination, because of its
exaggeration and false association of Gothic-
romantic ideas with reality, is invariably the
locus of deception.

II

     Complementing the broad parody of the imag-
ination in Northanger Abbey is Jane Austen's comic
representation of real life, which boldly draws
attention to the way character and behavior

actually or commonly appear, and not the way they
are imagined in fictional romances. Running
counter to the reader's expectations, the comic-
realistic narrative of Catherine Morland's life
is an anti-romance, in which, as Johnson explains
in Rambler no. 4 "life /is exhibited7 in its true
state, diversified only by accidents that daily
happen in the world, and influenced by passions
and qualities which are really to be found in
conversing with mankind" (Works, III, 19). "No
one who had ever seen Catherine Morland in her
infancy," Jane Austen opens her anti-romance,
"would have supposed her born to be an heroine"
(NA, 14). Not only are her family ordinary and
"plain matter-of-fact people" who experience the
"common feelings of common life," Catherine herself has "by nature nothing heroic about her."
Her father is not a domestic tyrant, and her
mother did not die--after the fashion of romances--
in childbirth. Catherine is not beautiful, and
she is not prodigiously accomplished. There is
no heroic youth in the neighborhood to fall in
love with, no young lord, foundling, squire's son,
no ward brought up in her family.[16] Catherine's
entry into the public life of Bath, moreover, is
marked by nothing unusual or romantic. At her
first dance, she is not, in the hyperbolical
language of romance, called "a divinity" by anyone (NA, 23). Her first conversation with Henry
Tilney in the Lower Rooms involves "such matters
as naturally arose from the objects around them"
(NA, 25). Her conversation with Eleanor Tilney
involves "commonplace chatter," and Eleanor's
manner during this exchange shows none of the
"exaggerated feelings of extatic delight or in-
conceivable vexation on every trifling occurrence"
(NA, 56-57).

For all Catherine's impressionability to her
friend Isabella's affectations and recommended
reading, she realistically possesses a common degree of common sense. When Catherine sees Mr.
Tilney speaking with a fashionable, attractive
young woman, who is leaning on his arm, for
example, she immediately assumes the woman is his
sister, thus losing, in a characteristically anti-

heroic manner, "a fair opportunity of considering
him lost to her for ever, by being married already."
Jane Austen comically contrasts the falsifying
romance version of such a situation with the realistic version, founded on probabilities and facts:

> Guided only by what was simple and
> probable, it had never entered her head
> that Mr. Tilney could be married; he
> had not behaved, he had not talked,
> like the married men to whom she had
> been used; he had never mentioned a
> wife, and he had acknowledged a sister.
> From these circumstances sprang the
> instant conclusion of his sister's now
> being by his side; and therefore, instead
> of turning of a deathlike paleness, and
> falling in a fit on Mrs. Allen's bosom,
> Catherine sat erect, in the perfect use
> of her senses, and with cheeks only a
> little redder than usual. (NA, 53)

Often, in fact, guided not by her active imagination but by what is "simple and probable," by
"circumstances," by observation and remembrance,
and by the "perfect use of her senses," Catherine's
life is used to demonstrate, as Jane Austen says,
that "strange things may be generally accounted
for if their cause be fairly searched out" (NA,
16). Hence, after a bewildering and short-lived
excursion among the fantasies of romance at
Northanger Abbey, Catherine resolves to act with
"the greatest good sense" and learns to accept
realistically the "anxieties of common life" instead of the "alarms of romance" (NA, 201). When
General Tilney dismisses her from the abbey,
having learned of her ordinary background,
Catherine realizes that the anxiety thus caused
is "mournfully superior in reality and substance"
than any she has encountered in Mrs. Radcliffe's
romances, for it has "foundation in fact" and "in
probability." With her mind now focused on
"actual and natural evil," she returns to her home
in a hack post-chaise "without /heroic7 accident
or alarm." A "probable circumstance" (Eleanor's
marriage to a man of fortune placates the General's

greed) facilitates her wedding with Henry (NA, 250). And Henry's affection for Catherine, we are told, has originated in "nothing better than gratitude" for Catherine's affection for him. "It is a new circumstance in romance, and dreadfully derogatory of an heroine's dignity," Jane Austen comically reminds us, "but if it be as new in common life, the credit of a wild imagination will at least be all my own" (NA, 243).

The comic realism in Northanger Abbey serves an obvious moral purpose, best described in Johnson's Rambler no. 4, which discusses novels that "serve as lectures of conduct, and introductions into life" (Works, III, 21). Unlike romances, in which "every transaction and sentiment /is/ so remote from all that passes among men, that the reader /is/ in very little danger of making any applications to himself" and in which "virtues and crimes /are/ equally beyond his sphere of activity," novels which portray the life of an adventurer who is "levelled with the rest of the world" and who "acts in such scenes of the universal drama, as may be the lot of any other man" can be morally instructive:

> The purpose of these writings is surely not only to show mankind, but to provide that they may be seen hereafter with less hazard; to teach the means of avoiding the snares which are laid by Treachery for Innocence, without infusing any wish for that superiority with which the betrayer flatters his vanity; to give the power of counteracting fraud, without the temptation to practise it; to initiate youth by mock encounters in the art of necessary defence, and to increase prudence without impairing virtue. (Works, III, 22-23)

The "mock encounters" which the innocent Catherine experiences in her relationships with her false friends, the Thorpes, and with General Tilney illuminate for her and for the reader at once that real people are more complex than imaginary heroes and that real life situations ironically can be more deceptive and treacherous than those encountered in fiction.

That Catherine is the innocent in this moral paradigm is evident from her naive, uninformed responses to lifelike situations. When she first leaves home, she goes "looking forward to pleasures untasted and unalloyed, and free from the apprehension of evil as from the knowledge of it" (NA, 237). And almost at the close of her story, Henry is referring to Catherine when he asks Eleanor to be ready to welcome a sister-in-law who is "open, candid, artless, guileless, with affections strong but simple, forming no pretensions, and knowing no disguise" (NA, 206). At every turn in her development, Catherine displays her innocence, as when with childlike simplicity, she tells John Thorpe, "To marry for money I think the wickedest thing in existence" (NA, 124). Estimating character and behavior in terms of her own naive imagination, she innocently imputes nothing but good nature to the impudent, conceited, and disingenuous Thorpe and to his selfish, shrewd, and calculating sister Isabella; and for a while she is completely deceived by the smooth social hypocrisy and mercenariness of General Tilney.

Catherine and the reader alike learn two significant lessons from her encounters with the Thorpes and General Tilney. Both learn what Johnson calls the "art of necessary defence" against the real fraudulence and treachery of human society. More significantly, their introduction to the ways of the world teaches them that human nature is more complex and difficult to understand than one naively imagines.[17] They both recognize, to use Johnson's words, the limits of "virtues and crimes" that exist within a probable "sphere of /human/ activity" (Rambler 4, Works, III, 21). For a time both Catherine and the reader mistakenly believe, for example, that the General is one of those "unnatural and overdrawn" characters of the imagination, who are represented in fictional romances like The Mysteries of

Udolpho, and who are capable of unalloyed evil
(NA, 181). But, as Dr. Johnson observes, "to
imagine that every one who is not completely good
is irrecoverably abandoned, is to suppose that all
are capable of the same degree of excellence; it
is indeed to exact, from all, that perfection
which none can attain" (Rambler 70, Works, IV, 6).
Catherine's awakening into the real world of experience gives the lie to this imaginary assumption:

> Charming as were all Mrs. Radcliffe's
> works, and charming even as were the
> works of all her imitators, it was not
> in them perhaps that human nature, at
> least in the midland counties of England,
> was to be looked for. . . . Among the
> Alps and Pyrenees, perhaps, there were
> no mixed characters. There, such as
> were not spotless as an angel, might
> have the dispositions of a fiend. But
> in England it was not so; among the
> English, she believed, in their hearts
> and habits, there was a general though
> unequal mixture of good and bad. Upon
> this conviction, she would not be sur-
> prized if even in Henry and Eleanor
> Tilney, some slight imperfection might
> hereafter appear; and upon this convic-
> tion she need not fear to acknowledge
> some actual specks in the character of
> their father, who, though cleared from
> the grossly injurious suspicions which
> she must ever blush to have entertained,
> she did believe, upon serious consider-
> ation, to be not perfectly amiable. (NA,
> 200)

Though there is much irony at Catherine's expense,
in believing that unnatural characters may yet
live in the Alps and Pyrenees, Catherine's reflections, thoroughly consistent with her unso-
phisticated character, nevertheless represent a
major advance in her moral education. Catherine
comically acquires the Johnsonian view that the
"heroes and traitors, deliverers and persecutors"

of imaginary romances are really "beings of another
species" whose actions are "regulated upon motives
of their own, and who /have7 neither faults nor
excellencies in common" with humanity (Rambler, 4,
Works, III, 21). Recognizing through experience
the complexity of human character and behavior,
Catherine, as well as the reader of Northanger
Abbey, learns that real people are not usually
murderers, but are more frequently mercenary,
cunning, hypocritical and vain--and sometimes, as
with Eleanor and Henry, even habitually, though
not perfectly, good.

Common sense, experience, and observation,
then, are ultimately what rescue Catherine Morland
and the reader from the illusory world of the imagination, and restore them to a sobering apprehension of reality. To say more than this--that Jane
Austen's irony, directed primarily against the
active imagination and the Gothic-sentimental
romances that nurture it, turns upon itself to
undercut even the direct experience of sensory
reality--is to misrepresent the Lockean epistemology upon which her parody is built, and to
misconstrue her evident moral intention. In
Northanger Abbey, Jane Austen narrates the richly
amusing story of an ingenue encountering and
learning from the deceptions of the real world;
with a traditional moral purpose and an eighteenth-
century epistemology she achieves a complex fusion
of bold parody and broad comic-realism.

Worldly deceptions, of course, Jane Austen
handles with more artistic dexterity in Mansfield
Park, where another ingenue, Fanny Price, encounters the treachery of a set of characters far
more complex and cunning than those who for a time
deceive Catherine Morland. But, again, unless he
recognizes the Johnsonian moral lessons which inform Mansfield Park, the reader himself will be
deceived--as many critics seem to have been--by
those characters of worldly charm and grace, whom
Johnson would have aptly described as "splendidly
wicked /people7, whose endowments threw a bright-
ness on their crimes" (Rambler 4, Works, III, 23).

NOTES

[1]A. Walton Litz, _Jane Austen: A Study of Her Artistic Development_ (New York: Oxford Univ. Press, 1965), p. 63.

[2]Andrew H. Wright, _Jane Austen's Novels: A Study in Structure_ (New York: Oxford Univ. Press, 1967), p. 96.

[3]Alistair M. Duckworth, _The Improvement of the Estate: A Study of Jane Austen's Novels_ (Baltimore: The Johns Hopkins Press, 1971), p. 98.

[4]Wright, p. 102; Duckworth, p. 99; Litz, p. 63. Raymond D. Havens, "Johnson's Distrust of the Imagination," _ELH_, 10 (1943), 246, notes that Johnson "never assigns to /the imagination/ the profoundly important role which Blake, Coleridge, and Wordsworth attributed to it by virtue of its creative, plastic or modifying, and unifying or 'esemplastic' power. Nor is there any suggestion that the imagination is a means of insight into truth."

[5]See Jean H. Hagstrum, _Samuel Johnson's Literary Criticism_ (1952; rpt. with new preface, Chicago: Univ. of Chicago Press, 1967), p. 7.

[6]John Locke, _Essay Concerning Human Understanding_, ed. Alexander Campbell Fraser (New York: Dover Publications, 1959), II, i, 24; hereafter cited as Locke, _Essay_.

[7]Locke, _Essay_, IV, i, 2.

[8]See _Jane Austen's Letters to Her Sister Cassandra and Others_, ed. R. W. Chapman, 2nd ed. (1952; rpt. London: Oxford Univ. Press, 1964), pp. 32-33, 49, 181.

[9]See Joseph Wood Krutch, _Samuel Johnson_ (New York: Holt, 1944), p. 322.

34

[10]Quoted in Kenneth MacLean, John Locke and English Literature of the Eighteenth Century (1936; rpt. New York: Russell and Russell, 1962), pp. 55-56.

[11]Locke, Essay, II, xxx, 2.

[12]Locke, Essay, II. xxxiii, 4.

[13]Locke, Essay, II, xxxiii, 5.

[14]Locke, Essay, II, xxxiii, 10.

[15]See, for example, Litz, p. 64.

[16]See also Alan D. McKillop, "Critical Realism in Northanger Abbey," in Ian Watt, ed., Jane Austen: A Collection of Critical Essays (Englewood Cliffs, N.J.: Prentice-Hall, 1963), p. 56.

[17]See also Kenneth L. Moler, Jane Austen's Art of Allusion (Lincoln: Univ. of Nebraska Press, 1968), pp. 28-31.

CHAPTER III

HARDSHIP, RECOLLECTION, AND DISCIPLINE:
THREE LESSONS IN MANSFIELD PARK

A stubborn critical question for readers of
Mansfield Park is whether Jane Austen's overt
moral purpose interferes with her creation of
character. In a very influential early essay on
the novel, Reginald Farrer charged that Jane
Austen's didacticism is "always at cross-purposes"
with the characters whom she creates, that the
heroine is "the most terrible incarnation we have
of the female prig-pharisee," and consequently,
that Mansfield Park is "vitiated throughout by a
radical dishonesty."[1] Adverse criticism has
hardly abated since Farrer's time, but the misleading assumption of much of it is that the
traditional morality affirmed in Mansfield Park
is somehow untransformed material which sticks
out of the otherwise organic texture of the novel,
and which does not, in the Jamesian sense at
least, artistically determine incident or illus-
trate character.[2] Certainly Jane Austen teaches
some difficult moral lessons in Mansfield Park:
that recollection of principle is the basis of
moral judgment, that discipline brings theoretical
principle into practice, and that unavoidable
hardship, suffering, and sacrifice strengthen
moral character. But Jane Austen does not instruct at the expense of characterization; on the
contrary, she ironically integrates her instruction in dramatic moments that reveal or expose
the moral status of her characters. If we illuminate these dramatic moments and trace in them
the central lessons of Mansfield Park, we may
finally recognize that Fanny Price is indeed a
formidable moral figure, not because she is prig-
gish or pharisaical, but rather because, by contrast, her cousins and their London friends are
morally unprincipled. We may acknowledge, too,
that if Fanny is finally rewarded with happiness,
she has through her recollection, discipline, and
voluntary sacrifice earned it; and that if Maria

Bertram and Henry and Mary Crawford are not so
rewarded, they through habitual forgetfulness,
idleness, and selfishness have not deserved it.
Ultimately, we may realize that the alleged conflict between Jane Austen's art and her morality
is more apparent than real.

The moral principles embodied in Mansfield
Park, as in all of Jane Austen's novels, are con-
sonant with orthodox eighteenth-century English
Christianity, exemplified in such diverse sources
as the Anglican Book of Common Prayer, the Tatler
and Spectator periodicals, and the innumerable
conduct books and sermons written throughout the
century. Traditional concepts--like the importance
of self-knowledge and the repudiation of pride,
of rational self-control, of practical common
sense, and of discipline, duty and sacrifice--
are pervasive in these documents, but nowhere do
they find a more comprehensive expression than in
the work of "the first moralist of the age," Dr.
Samuel Johnson.3 In Mansfield Park Jane Austen
refers to Johnson favorably by name, and she de-
notes her approval of his part in Fanny's training
by placing a volume of his Idler essays in Fanny's
room. More importantly, she underlines in oblique
allusions to a grim but realistic Johnson--as in
her affirmation of "the advantages of early hardship and discipline, and the consciousness of
being born to struggle and endure"--their mutual
conviction in the importance of a religious and
moral education (MP, 473). Jane Austen affirms
in Fanny's life what Johnson declared in the pages
of the Adventurer: "To strive with difficulties,
and to conquer them, is the highest human felicity; the next, is to strive, and deserve to conquer" (Adventurer I11, Works, II, 455).

The extent of Fanny's hardship and struggle
is suggested shortly after Sir Thomas Bertram's
decision to assume responsibility for rearing and
educating his poor relation at Mansfield Park.
From the time of Fanny's arrival at the home of
the baronet, the social proprieties that separate
her from her aristocratic cousins are strictly
observed. At Mrs. Norris' suggestion, Fanny is

given a small attic bedroom, which is distant
from the rooms of the Bertram children and which
is unattended by their maidservants. At first,
the neglected young Fanny spends many days alone
crying on the attic stairs or sobbing herself to
sleep, for while "nobody meant to be unkind . . .
nobody put themselves out of their way to secure
her comfort" (MP, 14). Then, when her aunts
Bertram and Norris overwork her as an errand girl
and companion and her cousin Edmund overlooks her
to enjoy the more lively company of Mary Crawford,
Fanny finds herself "struggling against discontent"
(MP, 74). During the rehearsal of the play, she
is again neglected and retreats to the quiet of
her room, but even here there are always reminders
of some "former affliction" (MP, 152). She patiently endures the insults of her Aunt Norris
who, with meager understanding, regularly taunts
Fanny as an outsider and exhorts her to remember
her place: "Remember, wherever you are, you must
always be the lowest and last" (MP, 221). Fanny
quietly submits to this derision, as she submits
to the discomfort of a room without a fire. The
severities, privations, and restrictions that are
imposed on Fanny's life, however, are not without
a salutary effect. Fanny's patient acceptance of
them secures her from the querulousness, jealousy,
and discord that rack the luxurious lives of her
cousins and their friends, for as Johnson soberly
reminds us in the Rambler no. 150: "By suffering
willingly what we cannot avoid, we secure ourselves
from vain and immoderate disquiet" (Works, V, 33).
At Mansfield Park Fanny Price fully learns the
meaning of this lesson; characteristically, there
is "no spirit of murmuring within her" (MP, 280).

    Fanny's life of hardship and struggle, unlike
her cousins' life of ease and elegance, strengthens
her moral sensitivity. An early comparison between this affectionate, though shy, heroine of
ten and her spiteful, undisciplined cousins, Maria
and Julia, dramatically distinguishes their moral
sensibilities. Although Fanny can read and write,
she knows none of the elegant decorums which her
cousins have learned so well. Cruelly calling
Fanny "ignorant of many things with which they

39

had been long familiar," Maria and Julia believe
she is "prodigiously stupid," and continually
ridicule her and run to Lady Bertram and Mrs.
Norris with some fresh proof of Fanny's "stupid-
ity" (MP, 18). Either Fanny cannot put the map
of Europe together, or she does not know the
principal rivers of Russia, or she has never heard
of Asia Minor. She cannot distinguish between
water-colors and crayons, she is unable to repeat
the chronological order of the kings of England
and of the Roman emperors, and she is unaware of
a great deal of classical mythology, metallurgy,
planets, and philosophers--knowledge which is
encyclopedic and readily obtained by turning to a
reference book. Having come from a relatively
impoverished home, Fanny understandably lacks this
kind of knowledge, but she is certainly not incapable of acquiring it. Moreover, she is presently far more capable than her cousins of recollecting moral principle to judge right from wrong.
This capacity is gradually revealed as the novel
unfolds. For the moment, Mrs. Norris' flattering
response to her favorite nieces ironically penetrates the crucial difference between the children:
"Very true, indeed, my dears, but you are blessed
with wonderful memories, and your poor cousin has
probably none at all. There is a vast deal of
difference in memories, as well as in every thing
else, and therefore you must make allowance for
your cousin, and pity her deficiency" (MP, 19).
Unaware of the irony of her observation, Mrs.
Norris alludes to a familiar assumption in the
moral literature of the eighteenth century, namely,
that the memory makes of man a moral being. Dr.
Johnson, for instance, maintains in the Rambler
no. 41 that the ability of the mind to remember
is a "strong proof of the superior and celestial
nature of the soul of man," for as he carefully
explains:

          Memory is the purveyor of reason,
     the power which places those images be-
     fore the mind upon which the judgment
     is to be exercised, and which treasures
     up the determinations that are once
     passed, as the rules of future action,

or grounds of subsequent conclusions.
It is, indeed, the faculty of
remembrance, which may be said to place
us in the class of moral agents. If we
were to act only in consequence of some
immediate impulse, and receive no direction from internal motives of choice,
we should be pushed forward by an invinc-
ible fatality, without power or reason
for the most part to prefer one thing to
another, because we could make no comparison but of objects which might both
happen to be present. (Works, III, 223)

Jane Austen's narrative irony, therefore, runs
deep in Mrs. Norris' comparison of the children,
because although Maria and Julia have been edu-
cated thoroughly in feminine "accomplishments,"
although their minds have been swollen with need-
less information, although they continue "to
exercise their memories, practise their duets,
and grow tall and womanly," their intellectual
and moral life is stunted (MP, 20). Under Edmund's
tutelage, however, Fanny's intellectual and moral
life begins to grow. Fanny, unlike Maria and
Julia, develops a life abundantly filled with
recollections which enrich her experiences and
guide her moral judgments.

Some of Fanny's early recollections come to
light after the death of Mr. Norris. Sir Thomas
seizes this opportunity to relieve himself of the
full burden of Fanny's education by asking his
sister-in-law to accept Fanny as a permanent
household guest and companion. A quiet, though
dramatic, pause in the movement of the novel
occurs at this time, as Fanny gratefully and sadly
recalls the kindnesses she has already received
from the Bertrams and especially from Edmund. She
wonders how she will ever be able to thank Edmund
sufficiently, and she assures him that she will
"remember" his goodness always (MP, 26). Edmund
sympathetically replaces her fears with hopes that
he indeed shall be "remembered," since the distance separating them will be small and since they

will therefore see each other as much as ever.
Their conversation then turns to Fanny's fond
reminiscences of Edmund's part in her daily exercise. "Ah! cousin, when I remember how much I
used to dread riding," she exclaims, "what terrors
it gave me to hear it talked of as likely to do
me good" (MP, 27). Fanny can never forget that
Edmund patiently reasoned her out of her fears,
and convinced her that riding would benefit her
and that she would gradually grow to enjoy it.
Such solicitude Mrs. Norris has no intention of
devoting to Fanny or to her niece's education.
With barely enough money to support her as a
gentlewoman, and to enable her to live so as not
to disgrace the "memory" of her deceased husband,
she declines Sir Thomas' proposal and hypocrit-
ically reminds the Bertrams that she must struggle
through her own sorrows and difficulties alone.
Mrs. Norris will keep a spare bedroom in her
cottage for any friend who may happen to visit
her, yet she simply has no room for Fanny. Nor
does she have any recollection of her own prom-
ises to assist the Bertrams in the education of
Fanny when she privately explains to her sister,
"My sole desire is to be of use to your family"
(MP, 30).

     That Fanny's memory alone has deepened and
matured becomes increasingly--and ironically--
clear when we recognize that her cousins and the
Crawfords have either clouded their recollections
or cultivated no memory at all. To Maria Bertram,
for example, marriage to Mr. Rushworth is desirable only because it will secure her a larger
income than her father's and a home in London.
With no small irony, the narrator observes that
it gradually became by "rule of moral obligation,
her evident duty to marry Mr. Rushworth if she
could" (MP, 38). Mary Crawford, too, remembers
only a cynical maxim for marriage. "What is this
/marriage/, but a take in?" she flippantly asks
her sister, Mrs. Grant (MP, 46). Later, in a
conversation about the improvement of Sotherton
estate, Mr. Rushworth--turning to Maria--mentions
the road that leads from the west front of the
building to the top of the hill; but Maria va-

cantly replies, "The avenue! Oh! I do not rec-
ollect it. I really know very little of Sotherton"
(MP, 56). Fanny, however, "attentively listening"
close by, wonders in a low voice, "Cut down the
avenue! What a pity! Does not it make you think
of Cowper? 'Ye fallen avenues, once more I mourn
your fate unmerited.'" Moments of the past sink
deeply into Fanny's memory. Fanny innocently believes it would be delightful to oversee and then
remember the progress of renovation; but Maria
Bertram is completely uninterested, and Mary
Crawford wants no part of the work involved either.
On still other occasions, we recognize the depth
of Fanny's recollection, which is the core of her
growing moral character. When the horse on which
Fanny has taken daily exercise is carelessly over-
worked by Mary for her own pleasure, Fanny stands
alone in the distance and watches her ride longer
than the horse has been used to. Fanny, we are
told, begins to pity the abused horse: "If she
were forgotten the poor mare should be remembered"
(MP, 68). Again, when Edmund temporarily neglects
his vigilance over Fanny's health, Fanny laments
that "his own forgetfulness of her was worse than
any thing which /Lady Bertram and Aunt Norris/
had done" to her (MP, 74).

The importance of memory in the growth of
moral character assumes a somewhat larger dimension in the expedition to Sotherton. At the beginning of the journey, Maria is jealous and tac-
iturn because her sister, not she, is riding with
Henry Crawford. Maria's silence, however, is no
loss to Fanny, who is really not interested in
conversation with her cousin, since Fanny's "own
thoughts and reflections were habitually her best
companions" (MP, 80). Indeed, we are told that
"in observing the appearance of the country, the
bearings of the roads, the difference of soil,
the state of the harvest, the cottages, the
cattle, the children, she found entertainment that
could only have been heightened by having Edmund
to speak to of what she felt." Echoes of the
eighteenth-century moral heritage can be heard in
these narrative observations, for as Dr. Johnson
affirms in the Rambler no. 5, the man who "enlarges

his curiosity after the works of nature demonstrably multiplies the inlets of happiness." Elaborating on this thought, Johnson maintains:

A man that has formed this habit of turning every new object to his entertainment, finds in the productions of nature an inexhaustible stock of materials upon which he can employ himself, without any temptations to envy or malevolence; faults, perhaps, seldom totally avoided by those, whose judgment is much exercised upon the works of art. He has always a certain prospect of discovering new reasons for adoring the sovereign author of the universe, and probable hopes of making some discovery of benefit to others, or of profit to himself. (Works, III, 28-29)

Like the person in Johnson's essay, Fanny is presently absorbed in the works of nature, while Maria, sitting beside her in the carriage, is angry and jealous, bored with the country journey, and totally unable to open her mind to a world that might enlarge her moral consciousness. Mary Crawford, too, shows no appreciation for the sublimity of nature and the tranquilizing reflections it may engender. Mary, in fact, "saw nature, inanimate nature, with little observation; her attention was all for men and women, her talents for the light and lively" (MP, 81).

The word "attention," in this context, signals an activity of the mind which precedes and assists the memory. John Locke, whose Essay Concerning Human Understanding represents the prevailing eighteenth-century psychology, acknowledges that "attention and repetition help much to the fixing any ideas in the memory."[4] Dr. Johnson similarly recognizes the psychological importance of attention in the development of memory. In the Idler no. 74, for example, he considers a worthy method of sharpening the memory while reading:

44

The true art of memory is the art
of attention. No man will read with
much advantage, who is not able, at
pleasure, to evacuate his mind, or who
brings not to his author an intellect
defecated and pure, neither turbid with
care nor agitated by pleasure. If the
repositories of thought are already full,
what can they receive? If the mind is
employed on the past or future, the book
will be held before the eyes in vain.
What is read with delight is commonly
retained, because pleasure always secures attention; but the books which
are consulted by occasional necessity,
and perused with impatience, seldom
leave any traces on the mind. (Works,
II, 232)

This specific advice for remembering what is read
can certainly be extended to the remembrance of
all human experience. Attention is necessary if
the mind is to retain aùd recall what it experiences.

That Fanny is an extraordinarily attentive
young woman, that she is sensitive to the perception of experience, is a clear sign of her
expanding moral consciousness. At the Sotherton
estate, for instance, Fanny and Mary Crawford are
both escorted by Mrs. Rushworth, but between the
two young ladies there is "no comparison in the
willingness of their attention, for Miss Crawford,
who had seen scores of great houses, and cared
for none of them had only the appearance of
civilly listening, while Fanny, to whom every
thing was almost as interesting as it was new,
attended with unaffected earnestness" (MP, 85).
Fanny, unlike Mary, is simply fascinated by the
history and long tradition of the Rushworth
family; her imagination is warmed with "scenes
of the past." Mary herself recognizes her companion's attentiveness, and fully understands why
Fanny should be so tired after the tour, for as
she comments, "There is nothing in the course of

one's duties so fatiguing as what we have been doing this morning--seeing a great house, dawdling from one room to another--straining one's eyes and one's attention" (MP, 95-96). Mrs. Rushworth informs her guests, when they reach the chapel, that prayers were formerly read in it by the domestic chaplain--"within the memory of many," but Mary Crawford irreverently remarks that the termination of the practice was probably an "improvement" (MP, 86). To her mind "the obligation of attendance, the formality, the restraint, the length of time"--all of these are formidable obstacles to prayer and reflection. Both Fanny and Edmund, however, are visibly disappointed in the discontinuance of the practice; Edmund even challenges Mary's preference of private devotions to public prayers, and asks her if she thinks a mind which is permitted to wander in a chapel would be more collected in a closet. Mary foolishly thinks so, for as she rationalizes, "there would be less to distract the attention from without, and it would not be tired so long" (MP, 88). But "the mind which does not struggle against itself under one circumstance," Edmund courageously replies, "would find objects to distract it in the other."

Mary Crawford is apparently incapable of focusing her attention in any disciplined or self-sacrificing way. It is only after Henry, Julia, and Maria's departure from Mansfield Park, for example--when there is no one else to talk with--that she cultivates Fanny's companionship. Mary frequently invites Fanny to visit her at the parsonage, and Fanny is "obliged to submit to all this attention" (MP, 206). While the two ladies are sitting in Mrs. Grant's garden on one of these visits, Fanny looks around herself at the shrubbery and is visibly affected by its growth and beauty. She remembers how only three years before there was nothing but a hedgerow along the upper side of the field, never appreciated, "never /like her, we assume/ thought of as any thing, or capable of becoming any thing" (MP, 208). She sees that it has now been turned into a walk, although she does not know whether it is "most

valuable as a convenience /like her/ or an orna-
ment." "Perhaps," she wonders, "in another three
years we may be forgetting--almost forgetting what
it was before." Her reverie heightens into a
rhapsody on the changes of the human mind:

> "How wonderful, how very wonderful the
> operations of time, and the changes of
> the human mind!" And following the
> latter train of thought, she soon after-
> wards added: "If any one faculty of our
> nature may be called more wonderful than
> the rest, I do think it is memory. There
> seems something more speakingly incompre-
> hensible in the powers, the failures,
> the inequalities of memory, than in any
> other of our intelligences. The memory
> is sometimes so retentive, so service-
> able, so obedient--at others, so bewil-
> dered and so weak--and at others again,
> so tyrannic, so beyond controul!--We are
> to be sure a miracle every way--but our
> powers of recollecting and of forgetting,
> do seem peculiarly past finding out."
> (MP, 208-209)[5]

Fanny's sensitive observations are something of a
conversational cul-de-sac; they lead nowhere in
the conversation between Fanny and Mary Crawford,
who is described by the author as "untouched and
inattentive." The conversation then resumes along
other lines, not because the subject is unimportant, but rather because the point has been sufficiently made--Mary Crawford is uninterested and
inattentive to the faculty which places man in
the class of moral agents.

There is more than a suggestion in Mansfield
Park that those characters who are not endowed--
as Fanny is--with a strong awareness of the past
and who do not exercise the faculty of memory are
morally irresponsible. Henry Crawford's dis-
armingly superficial conversation with Maria
Bertram, for example, in which they discuss the
prospects of Sotherton and its improvement, res-

onates with moral significance. Smiling at Maria
(who is engaged to Mr. Rushworth), Henry insin-
uates that he shall never see Sotherton with so
much pleasure as he does now. Momentarily em-
barrassed by Henry's obvious intentions, Maria
deflects his attention by reminding him that he
is "too much a man of the world not to see with
the eyes of the world" and that if other people
find Sotherton improved he will also (MP, 98).
Yet Henry ironically replies, "My feelings are
not quite so evanescent, nor my memory of the
past under such easy dominion as one finds to be
the case with men of the world." His reply is
followed by a short silence, and then the conversation turns to the ride to the Rushworth estate,
Maria reminding him that he seemed by his laughter
to enjoy the drive with Julia very much. "Yes, I
believe we were /laughing/," he responds with
indifference, "but I have not the least recollection at what." Henry has no strong recollections.
That is certainly why no moral scruples prevent
his later elopement with another man's wife.

With such meager recollection, it is small
wonder that when the question of performing the
theatrical Lovers' Vows arises, many of the characters are unable to judge its suitability for
presentation. By their judgment only Fanny and
Edmund discern the circumstantial impropriety of
acting at this time.[6] Edmund advises against the
play for two reasons--first, because it would
show "great want of feeling" on his father's
account, whose life is in constant danger in another part of the world, and second, because (as
the play involves the sentimental and sensational
tale of illegitimacy and seduction) it would be
"imprudent . . . with regard to Maria," who is
engaged to be married (MP, 125). But having no
recollection of principle at all, the others
merely ridicule Edmund's objections and Fanny's
scruples as too serious. They are certainly deficient in memory, "the purveyor of reason, the
power which places those images before the mind
upon which the judgment is to be exercised"
(Rambler 41, Works, III, 223).

48

Significantly, then, Fanny stands with Edmund
apart from her other cousins and the Crawfords
during the preparation of this play. Fanny herself retreats to the small East room where, apart
from the rest of the household, she finds solace
for the increasing alienation which the play has
caused her. With her plants and her books all
within reach, Fanny can scarcely see any object
in that room which has no "interesting remembrance
connected with it" (MP, 151-52). Though she has
often been ridiculed and neglected in the past,
every occurrence of either abuse has invariably
led to some consoling act. Lady Bertram may have
spoken kindly to her, her tutor may have been encouraging, or more frequently, Edmund may have
given her encouragement, affection, or instruction.
All of these meaningful moments are treasured in
Fanny's memory, where all is "so blended together,
so harmonized by distance." In this room she sits
down to think about the past, and to judge what
she ought to do in the present. She has been un-
justly accused of ingratitude by her Aunt Norris
for not cooperating in the theatrical scheme,
and Fanny's delicate conscience makes her weigh
the integrity of her own motives. She wonders
whether she is right in refusing to participate
in a project that would bring others so much
pleasure. Her mind then wanders to the small objects on the tables given to her as presents in
the past, and she becomes momentarily bewildered
by the "amount of the debt which all these kind
remembrances produced" (MP, 153). But the critical moment of judgment is deferred by Edmund's
sudden knock at the door. Having decided to compromise his own position by performing and thereby excluding outsiders from the play, he has come
to consult Fanny's opinion. Edmund immediately
realizes, from Fanny's reticence, that her
"judgment" is not with him. He leaves sadly, yet
before he does, he recognizes some of Fanny's
reading close at hand--George Crabbe's moral Tales
and a volume of Johnson's Idler essays. Supported
by her reading, by her reflection, and by her sensitive though strong memory, Fanny remains determined not to act.

Fanny indeed has a morally strong character, but not because her memory alone is strong. Principles once learned and subsequently recalled by the memory are of little value unless they are consistently acted upon. Sir Thomas Bertram learns this lesson after the tragic adulteries of his own children. Sir Thomas, we are told, "feared that principle, active principle, had been wanting, that they had never been properly taught to govern their inclinations and tempers, by that sense of duty which can alone suffice. They had been instructed theoretically in their religion, but never required to bring it into daily practice" (MP, 463). Behind Sir Thomas' recognition lies a strong moral tradition which insists upon the exercise of the intellectual and moral faculties. "The difference, so observable in men's understandings and parts," John Locke observes in his treatise Conduct of the Understanding, "does not arise so much from their natural faculties as acquired habits. . . . No body is made any thing by hearing of rules, or by laying them up in his memory; practice must settle the habit of doing without reflecting on the rule."[8] More immediately relevant to Mansfield Park, however, is the recurrence in Samuel Johnson's essays of the themes enjoining the exercise of moral principle. Johnson warns in the Idler no. 4, for example, that compassion will produce unlasting effects if it never settles into a "principle of action" (Works, II, 13). He speaks, in the Rambler no. 7, of the moral conquest of ourselves by developing "standing principles of action" (Works, III, 40). In the Idler no. 27, he argues that attempts to change patterns of behavior frequently fail because in the end "custom is commonly too strong for the most resolute resolver" and "habit prevails" (Works, II, 85). Nevertheless, he affirms our "duty to struggle" against the passions so we do not become oppressed by them (Adventurer 108, Works, II, 450). Realistically, he assures his readers that "custom is equally forcible to bad and good; nature will always be at variance with reason, but will rebel more feebly as she is oftener subdued." Since he is painfully aware that bad habits formed early in life are so great

that almost every man returns to them, he urges
"constant attention and unremitting exertion to
establish contrary habits of superior efficacy"
(Life, II, 366).

When we examine Fanny Price in the light of
this traditional lesson, we realize that her
moral character is molded by habit as much as by
recollection. From the time that she was brought
to Mansfield Park as a frail young girl, her education was supervised by Edmund, who guided her
daily riding exercises, and just as regularly
listened to her reading, recommended books for
her leisure hours, encouraged her taste and cor-
rected and heightened her powers of judgment.
The attentions which Edmund has showered on her
register a cumulative impression of habit in
Fanny's life, so that when--even for a brief
period--this routine is broken, we are fully conscious of its neglect.9 When, for example,
Fanny's old grey pony dies and she is deprived of
daily exercise, her health fails, because her Aunt
Norris one day urges her to walk "beyond her
strength" and on the next Lady Bertram keeps her
sitting at home without any exercise at all (MP,
36). With Edmund's resolute declaration to his
aunts that "Fanny must have a horse," we infer
that only through the daily habit of riding in
the country air will her health regain tolerable
vigor. Similarly, when Fanny is later confined
in the cramped quarters of her parents' home in
Portsmouth, she again begins "to feel the effect
of being debarred from her usual, regular exercise" (MP, 409).

Having learned the importance of habit in
her own life, Fanny grows to lament its absence
in the lives of others. She regrets the discon-
tinuation of the custom of regular public prayer
at Sotherton, and rather innocently exclaims:
"There is something in a chapel and chaplain so
much in character with a great house, with one's
ideas of what such a household should be! A
whole family assembling regularly for the purpose
of prayer, is fine!" (MP, 86). Mary Crawford,
however, scoffs at the idea of regular prayer,

51

and she is duly warned by Edmund about the weakness of a mind which "grow/s̶/ into a habit from neglect" (MP, 87).

Like his sister Mary, Henry Crawford has no affinity for sound moral habits either. On the contrary, his behavior is unstable, consistently irresponsible, and even provoking. On one of his evening visits to Sir Thomas' home, while Fanny has been patiently reading to Lady Bertram from Shakespeare, Henry picks up the volume of plays and begins reading aloud. Henry's reading is so accomplished that Fanny feels inclined to listen with considerable interest. Edmund, too, recognizes the excellence of Henry's delivery, and the two gentlemen begin to discuss the common neglect of reading--the "total inattention" to it--in the schools, and the inexperience of otherwise sensible and well-informed men, when suddenly called upon to read aloud. Together they cite numerous instances of rhetorical failures and blunders, and attribute them to their probable causes: "the want of management of the voice, of proper modulation and emphasis, of foresight and judgment, all proceeding from the first cause, want of early attention and habit" (MP, 339). With regret Edmund, who is soon to be ordained, observes that even within the clerical life, the art of reading is insufficiently studied. Henry of course wonders whether the effect of a liturgy which has such natural beauty can be destroyed even by a careless, slovenly reading and attention. Still, he adds, "I must confess being not always so attentive as I ought to be--(here was a glance at Fanny) that nineteen times out of twenty I am thinking how such a prayer ought to be read, and longing to have it to read myself" (MP, 340). Suddenly he thinks he can hear Fanny speak, but he is mistaken. "I fancied you might be going to tell me I ought to be more attentive, and not allow my thoughts to wander," he addresses her. But Fanny demurs, saying only that he knows his duty too well for her to remind him of it. Returning to the subject of sermons, then, Henry observes that the preacher who "rouses the attention" of his congregation without offending their

tastes or feelings is a man whom he would emulate.
If he were a clergyman, Henry blindly continues,
he would not be fond of preaching regularly.
"Now and then, perhaps," he explains, "once or
twice in the spring, after being anxiously expected for half a dozen Sundays together; but not
for a constancy; it would not do for a constancy"
(MP, 341). Fanny involuntarily shakes her head,
and Henry instantly rushes to her side entreating
to know why she disapproves:

> "You shook your head at my acknowl-
> edging that I should not like to engage
> in the duties of a clergyman always, for
> a constancy. Yes, that was the word.
> Constancy, I am not afraid of the word.
> I would spell it, read it, write it with
> any body. I see nothing alarming in the
> in the word. Did you think I ought?"

> "Perhaps, Sir," said Fanny, wearied
> at last into speaking--"perhaps, Sir, I
> thought it was a pity you did not always
> know yourself as well as you seemed to
> do at that moment." (MP, 343)

Henry is glad to have received some response from
her, even if it is one of disapproval. "You think
me unsteady--easily swayed by the whim of the
moment--easily tempted--easily put aside," he then
proudly announces, "but we shall see." Keenly
realizing that no amount of protest will convince
her otherwise, he boasts, "My conduct shall speak
for me--absence, distance, time shall speak for
me.--They shall prove, that as far as you can be
deserved by any body, I do deserve you." But
Henry's eventual elopement with Maria Rushworth
only thunders his inconstancy. Even Sir Thomas
presently harbors doubts about Henry's claims to
perseverance. Ironically, while Sir Thomas wishes
Henry to become a "model of constancy," he fully
recognizes that "the best means of effecting it
would be by not trying him too long" (MP, 345).

This emotionally tense moment in Mansfield
Park is relieved by Fanny's visit to her parents'

53

home in Portsmouth--an episode which facilitates
the climax of the novel (the respective elopements
of Henry with Maria and of Julia with Yates), the
elimination of Henry as a serious contender for
Fanny, the full exposure of Mary's character to
Edmund and Fanny, and the triumphant return of
Fanny to Mansfield Park. While Sir Thomas expects
Fanny to go to Portsmouth willingly, he also hopes
that her visit will make her "heartily sick of
home," and that an abstinence from the elegance
of Mansfield Park may incline her to a more sober
estimate of Henry Crawford and of the material
advantages of marrying him (MP, 369).

Fanny, of course, never yields to the illusory attractiveness of Henry Crawford; but her
visit does convince her that, as painful as her
life has been at Mansfield Park, it is still far
more desirable than life at Portsmouth. Fanny
realizes that life with her family is not what she
has expected, for the house is "the abode of noise,
disorder, and impropriety" (MP, 388). The
Portsmouth rooms are small and the walls are thin.
The servants are ill-managed, and the children
are continually arguing among themselves. Fanny's
father is negligent of his family, and "his habits
were worse, and his manners coarser" than she has
expected. Her mother spends her days in a slow
bustle--"always busy without getting on, always
behindhand and lamenting it, without altering her
ways; wishing to be an economist, without contrivance or regularity"--and she is continually
dissatisfied with her servants, and unable to
gain their respect (MP, 389). Throughout her
visit Fanny's memory calls to mind the full contrast between this house of "mismanagement and
discomfort" and her Mansfield home of "elegance,
propriety, regularity, harmony" (MP, 391). "In
a review of the two houses, as they appeared to
her before the end of a week," the narrator concludes, "Fanny was tempted to apply to them
Dr. Johnson's celebrated judgment as to matrimony
and celibacy, and say, that though Mansfield Park
might have some pains, Portsmouth could have no
pleasures" (MP, 392). This allusion to Rasselas,

recalling Johnson's grim assurance that "there is commonly discord" in all families, rich and poor alike, cannot be overlooked (R, xxvi, 67). Symbolically it demonstrates that the discord and deprivation which Fanny has experienced in both her natural and her adopted families are unavoidable. But while Fanny has suffered much at Mansfield Park, through the ill treatment of her aunts and the ridicule of her cousins, her discipline and moral strength have preserved her from discontentment and given her considerably more pleasure than she could ever find at Portsmouth. The comparison of one life filled with unendurable discord, contention, and misery, and another--sometimes rather painful--life made bearable and often pleasurable by discipline and fortitude, strengthens Fanny's attachment to Mansfield Park.

The appropriateness of Fanny's comparison of the two houses is supported by another moral lesson familiar in the eighteenth century, namely, that recalling the distress and misfortune of others makes us grateful for our own, far less miserable, circumstances. Johnson imparts this lesson in his Rambler no. 52:

> When we look abroad, and behold the
> multitudes that are groaning under
> evils heavier than those which we have
> experienced, we shrink back to our own
> state, and instead of repining that so
> much must be felt, learn to rejoice that
> we have not more to feel.

> By this observation of the miseries
> of others, fortitude is strengthened,
> and the mind brought to a more extensive
> knowledge of her own powers. As the
> heroes of action catch the flame from
> one another, so they to whom providence
> has allotted the harder task of suffering
> with calmness and dignity, may animate
> themselves by the remembrance of those
> evils which have been laid on others,
> perhaps naturally as weak as themselves,
> and bear up with vigour and resolution

against their own oppressions, when they
see it possible that more severe afflic-
tions may be born. (Works, III, 283)

We have already noted that Fanny's life, from the
time of her arrival at Mansfield Park, has been
a difficult struggle. Fanny has not simply en-
dured; she has also learned that to act with
resolution in times of hardship is easier than to
suffer. In the Portsmouth episode, the period of
her most difficult struggle, Fanny looks about
her for what Johnson elsewhere calls the "accidental benefits which prudence may confer on
every state" (Rambler 150, Works, V, 34), and she
finds consolation for the hardship of her family's
home in the growing knowledge of her younger
sister Susan and in the "hope of being of service
to her" (MP, 395).

Fanny's relationship with Susan not only confirms the importance of confronting, struggling
with, and ultimately surmounting unavoidable hardship, but it also underlines the significance of
discipline in the development of moral character.
In Portsmouth Fanny gradually discovers the full
effects of the neglect of education in the lives
of Mary and Henry Crawford. Such neglect, she
thoroughly realizes, must not be repeated in the
life of her younger sister.

Though Henry at this time seems to have improved his manners--traveling to Portsmouth to
demonstrate his affection for Fanny--his conduct
is largely a stratagem to win her approbation,
just as his securing William's promotion earlier
was an attempt to purchase her love. Henry's
education has provided him no steadiness of purpose
or manner, and he is therefore easily discouraged
by Fanny's apparent disinterest. Neglecting to
expedite justice in his tenant's claims in
Norfolk--which he deliberately tells Fanny he
proposes to do as his "duty" and in order to secure
"agreeable recollections for his own mind"--he
flirts instead with Maria Rushworth at Richmond
(MP, 404). When the news of his elopement with
Maria finally reaches Fanny, she fully recognizes

that he is simply incapable of being "steadily
attached to any one woman in the world" (MP, 438).

The neglect of discipline in Mary Crawford's
life, too, is completely disclosed to Fanny at
Portsmouth. Fanny has vaguely suspected all along
that Mary is toying with Edmund's affections, and
only proving in her return to London her lack of
seriousness by a corresponding "return to London
habits" (MP, 417). Mary betrays to Fanny the
superficiality of her attachment to Edmund, since
his "gentleman-like appearance" is the only estimable quality Mary can perceive. Edmund's subsequent letter to Fanny confirms this impression.
Disappointed in Mary's manner, he attributes her
worldliness to the "habits of wealth" and to
friends who have been "leading her astray for
years" (MP, 421). But Mary's own words speak
louder than Edmund's suspicions. In a final self-
exposure Mary writes to Fanny about Henry's elopement (the climax of his own unsteadiness), and
cooly urges her to hush up the affair. If only
Fanny had accepted Henry's proposal "as she ought,"
Mary later rationalizes, Henry would have been
"too happy and too busy to want any other object"
(MP, 456). She loosely argues that he would have
taken no pains to resume his affair with Mrs.
Rushworth: "It would have all ended in a regular
standing flirtation." With flirtation the only
"regular" mode of conduct she and Henry are really
capable of, their lives dramatically represent a
lack of moral discipline and a tremendous waste
of human potentiality. In Edmund's last encounter
with Mary, which he describes to Fanny, he imagines
that he saw in Mary's face "a mixture of many
feelings--a great, though short struggle--half a
wish of yielding to truths, half a sense of shame--
but," he remorsefully concludes, "habit, habit
carried it" (MP, 458). "Habit prevails," Samuel
Johnson soberly reminds us; "custom is commonly
too strong for the most resolute resolver."

Fanny's relationship with Susan, then, can
be seen only in the large context of moral education. The tragedy of Mary's and Henry's lives
must not be repeated in the life of Susan. Susan

Price must not be allowed to go her own way without direction, without life-sustaining recollections, and without sound moral habits. Sir Thomas may have sent Fanny to Portsmouth in order to appreciate by comparison the luxury of Mansfield Park, yet what Fanny learns to value most at his estate is not its affluence but the discipline by which her life has been enriched. Fanny sadly recognizes, too, that her mother and father lack any discipline and are therefore incapable of enriching their children's lives with the education they need.

At a particularly critical stage in her development, Susan sees much of what is wrong at home and wants to change it, but she lacks the moral courage and strength to do so. Her continual disagreements with her mother, her rash arguments with her brothers, and her petulance with her younger sister are all very distressing to Fanny, whose commingled compassion and respect for Susan embolden her efforts to rectify Susan's manners. Fanny attempts to teach her "the juster notions of what was due to every body, and what would be wisest for herself, which her own more favoured education had fixed in her" (MP, 396). She successfully intervenes in the argument Susan has had with Betsey over a small family keepsake, and increasingly observes an improvement in Susan's behavior.

The intimacy between the two sisters ultimately becomes a real mutual advantage. By sitting together upstairs they "avoided a great deal of the disturbance of the house; Fanny had peace, and Susan learnt to think it no misfortune to be quietly employed" (MP, 398). They sit without a fire, but "that was a privation familiar even to Fanny, and she suffered the less because reminded by it of the east-room." So powerful is Fanny's "remembrance of all her books and boxes, and various comforts" in her Mansfield room that she subscribes to a circulating library for Susan, who, because the "early habit of reading was wanting," has read nothing. Fanny longs to share with Susan her own first pleasures, and to inspire in her a taste for the reading she delighted in under Edmund's tutelage. She therefore devotes much attention to her sister, and Susan in turn becomes a "most attentive, profitable, thankful pupil" (MP, 418). Susan is eventually taken to Mansfield Park to replace Fanny, and in replication of Fanny's experience, she becomes for Lady Bertram the stationary servant niece Fanny once had been. Susan, like Fanny, is "soon welcome, and useful to all" (MP, 472). In the story of Susan Price, Jane Austen dramatically underlines the importance of hardship, recollection, and discipline in the development of moral character. She reiterates in the story of Susan Price the central lessons of Fanny's education--"the advantages of early hardship and discipline, and the consciousness of being born to struggle and endure" (MP, 473).

The moral lessons explored in Mansfield Park, therefore, do not interfere with Jane Austen's creation of character. In fact, they are the only sure measure of her artistic achievement, for without them we should be unable to recognize the ironies which illuminate in dramatic moments the moral status of her characters. Without the central lessons of Mansfield Park, we should be unable to appreciate sympathetically a heroine like Fanny Price, whose moral values stand unmistakably--and ironically--at the center of the novel. Though a precisian in her moral posture, Fanny is certainly no prig-pharisee. With sensitivity and recollection, strengthened by sound moral habit, and tempered under hardship and suffering, she--unlike her undisciplined cousins and their worldly London friends--is ideally prepared and finally rewarded for the moral judgments and personal sacrifices which life demands of her. Jane Austen, in other words, imposes no unjustified moral judgments on her characters, and she offers no unjust vindication of Fanny Price. Since her purpose of edification is perfectly at one with the characters whom she creates, morality in Jane Austen's fictional world is inseparable from her art.

In _Mansfield Park_ Johnsonian moral lessons
substantially illuminate Jane Austen's unified
development of characters, whose conduct expresses
or ironically exposes the state of their moral
education. But even an ideal moral education does
not eradicate the omnipresent means by which Jane
Austen's heroines may delude themselves, and
temporarily lose sight of what Edmund Bertram
calls "the most valuable knowledge . . . the
knowledge of ourselves and of our duty" (_MP_, 459).
Jane Austen's exploration of self-deception and
self-knowledge represents her Johnsonian frame of
reference in _Emma_ and _Pride and Prejudice_.

NOTES

[1]"Jane Austen," Quarterly Review, 228 (1917), 20, 22.

[2]Marvin Mudrick, for example, in Jane Austen: Irony as Defense and Discovery (1952; rpt. Berkeley: Univ. of California Press, 1968), p. 155, argues that the "thesis of Mansfield Park is severely moral: that one world, representing the genteel orthodoxy of Jane Austen's time, is categorically superior to any other. . . . To this thesis, everything else gives way: in the end, it subordinates or destroys every character." Joseph Duffy, "Moral Integrity and Moral Anarchy in Mansfield Park," ELH, 22 (1956), 71, similarly comments that Jane Austen's didacticism "manifests itself in a tactless display of sympathy and prejudice towards her characters, and it takes over completely in the concluding chapter when the novelist intrudes upon her created world, assumes a maddeningly pontifical air, and informs the reader of what might have been--if only certain individuals had known how to behave." A. Walton Litz, Jane Austen: A Study of Her Artistic Development (New York: Oxford Univ. Press, 1965), p. 130, claims that the "form of Mansfield Park expresses all too clearly its author's conviction that the values of art are not the ultimate ones."

[3]Robert Voitle, Samuel Johnson the Moralist (Cambridge, Mass.: Harvard Univ. Press, 1961), p. vii, is quoting the author of the "History of the Science of Morals" article, which appeared in the 1797 edition of the Encyclopaedia Britannica.

[4]Essay Concerning Human Understanding, ed. Alexander Campbell Fraser (New York: Dover Publications, 1959), II, x, 3.

[5]The traditional nature of Fanny's reflection may be demonstrated by comparing it with John Locke's observation (Essay Concerning Human Understanding, II, x, 5): "The memory of some men, it is true, is very tenacious, even to a miracle.

But yet there seems to be a constant decay of all
our ideas, even of those which are struck deepest,
and in minds the most retentive; so that if they
be not sometimes renewed, by repeated exercise of
the senses, or reflection on those kinds of objects which at first occasioned them, the print
wears out, and at last there remains nothing to
be seen. Thus the ideas, as well as children,
of our youth, often die before us: and our minds
represent to us those tombs to which we are
approaching; where, though the brass and marble
remain, yet the inscriptions are effaced by time,
and the imagery moulders away. The pictures
drawn in our minds are laid in fading colours;
and if not sometimes refreshed, vanish and dis-
appear."

[6]Although the critical literature on this
episode in Mansfield Park is extensive, no critic
has substantially improved upon R. W. Chapman's
assessment in Jane Austen: Facts and Problems
(1948; rpt. Oxford: Clarendon Press, 1950), p.
198, that the objections to the play are largely
topical. There is little evidence, for instance,
to justify Lionel Trilling's suggestion in
"Mansfield Park," The Opposing Self (New York:
Viking Press, 1955), p. 218, that on the question
of acting Jane Austen expresses a Platonic
distrust of assuming roles.

[7]Although Fanny refuses to act in the play,
she nevertheless finds pleasure in attending the
rehearsals and judging the quality of the actors'
performance. With exquisite irony, the narrator
comments, "As far as she /Fanny/ could judge,
Mr. Crawford was considerably the best actor of
all" (MP, 165). With equally keen irony, Fanny
charitably assists the foppish Mr. Rushworth, who
has been grumbling about the difficulty of learning
his lines. Everyone else believes he will have
every difficulty merely remembering the catchwords
to his speeches. But Fanny attempts to teach him
how to learn, giving him direction and "trying to
make an artificial memory for him" (MP, 166).

[8]Conduct of the Understanding, ed. Thomas
Fowler (Oxford: Clarendon Press, 1901), pp. 14-
15.

[9]That Mansfield Park covers the longest span
of time of all Jane Austen's novels is worth
remembering because only over this expanse of time
does the reader become fully conscious of the
exercise or neglect of moral principle.

CHAPTER IV

MARRIAGE AND SELF-KNOWLEDGE IN EMMA AND PRIDE AND PREJUDICE

Though often cited as the most formally perfect of Jane Austen's novels, Emma has provoked
critical responses which by implication question
the novel's form as well as its moral significance.
Dissatisfied with Emma's Electra-like marriage to
George Knightley, G. B. Stern complains, "Oh,
Miss Austen, it was not a good solution; it was
a bad solution, an unhappy ending, could we see
beyond the last pages of the book."[1] Similarly
disappointed, H. W. Garrod admits he is "a little
sorry for both parties when Emma marries Mr.
Knightley."[2] "And how 'happy' is the marriage,
with Knightley having to move into old Mr.
Woodhouse's establishment?" Mark Schorer rhetor-
ically asks. "Isn't it all, perhaps, a little
superficial--not the writing but the self-avowals
of the characters? A little perfunctory, as
comedy may be, telling us thereby that this is
comedy?"[3] For Edmund Wilson there is little
reason "to believe that /Emma's/ marriage with
Knightley would prevent her from going on as she
had done before."[4] Marvin Mudrick climaxes this
general critical dissatisfaction with the argument
that "the irony of Emma is multiple; and its
ultimate aspect is that there is no happy ending,
no easy equilibrium, if we care to project confirmed exploiters like Emma and Churchill into
the future of their marriages."[5]

Interestingly, several of these same critics
applaud the marriage of Elizabeth Bennet and
Darcy, in Pride and Prejudice; they affirm its
essential "rightness." Mudrick, for example,
claims that "what Elizabeth must choose, within
the bounds set by prudence, is an individual
equally complex" as herself, and that, of course,
is Darcy.[6] For Garrod their marriage happily
unites a "genuine Girl of Spirit" and a "genuine
Young Eligible."[7] To Schorer, Darcy and Elizabeth

represent respectively "aristocratic" and
"bourgeois" orders which "meet and conflict
and . . . merge"; their marriage somehow transcends
the attractiveness of each order.[8]

Contradictory interpretations of the conclusions to these novels may reflect in part the
difference of personality between Elizabeth Bennet
and Emma Woodhouse--a difference which Jane Austen
reminds us of in the letters: Elizabeth is "as
delightful a creature as ever appeared in print"
(Letters, 297), while Emma is "a heroine whom no
one but myself will much like."[9] Attracted by
the vitality, wit, and social rebelliousness of
Elizabeth, and repelled by the snobbishness,
condescension, and social manipulativeness of
Emma, we may applaud, on the basis of personality
alone, the marriage which Elizabeth so justly
deserves and question seriously whether Emma
either deserves Knightley or will improve under
his vigilant instruction. We fail to recognize,
however, the critical fact that both marriages
signal the end of a long and sinuous path of self-
deception both heroines have been treading, and
appropriately symbolize the proper degree of self-
knowledge which neither heroine has fully had
before. Both Elizabeth and Emma at the opening
of these novels are characterized by what
Christian moralists have perennially called the
sin of pride. Both are surpassingly confident of
being right, though in several ways they are surpassingly wrong, and both in the course of their
development are led to discover and regret their
errors of judgment and action. In this pattern
of moral development, Jane Austen reflects a
significant eighteenth-century interest in the
problem of self-knowledge and a particularly vital
topic of her favorite prose moralist, Samuel
Johnson, whose essays represent even in her life-
time the orthodox conception of character and of
moral growth. Without vitiating either the complexities of Jane Austen's characters or the substance of her moral frame of reference, we may
trace in the education of Elizabeth Bennet and
Emma Woodhouse characteristically Johnsonian

methods of recognizing and avoiding self-deception; in this exploration we may also discover why marriage is the most fitting symbol for their acquired self-knowledge.[10]

Self-knowledge, the attainment by one or more characters of what Edmund Bertram in Mansfield Park calls "the most valuable knowledge . . . the knowledge of ourselves and of our duty," is certainly a major theme in all of Jane Austen's novels (MP, 459). Yet self-knowledge is not the equivalent of modern notions of identity or of the meaning of one's existence in the mysteries of the universe. Self-knowledge refers, rather, to a precise recognition of the faults of temperament which impede the fulfillment of our known responsibilities in life.[11] A long tradition of moral literature preceding and contemporaneous with Jane Austen clarifies this definition of self-knowledge. But the significance of self-knowledge is nowhere more comprehensively explained than in the essays of Samuel Johnson. Reaffirming the ancient Greek precept "Be acquainted with thyself," Johnson declares that this lesson "comprise/s/ all the speculation requisite to a moral agent," for "every error in human conduct must arise from ignorance in ourselves, either perpetual or temporary" (Rambler 24, Works, III, 130, 131). As a representative practical moralist, Johnson does not simply insist on the importance of self-knowledge. Fully recognizing the difficulty of achieving self-knowledge, he explores extensively the "artifices of self-deceit," those expedients by which we lie, cheat, and impose upon ourselves to our own detriment (Rambler 8, Works, III, 43). In the Rambler no. 28, he enumerates some of these artifices: equating single acts of virtue with habitual practice, minimizing (by a remarkable twist of human reason) habitual faults as "casual failures, and single lapses," confounding the praise of goodness with the practice, and favorably comparing one's own moral life with one far worse (Works, III, 153).

Johnson's discussion of the arts of self-deceit, by which a man invariably persuades him-

self that he is better than he really is, suggests
that self-deceptions are ultimately forms of pride
and vanity. Indeed, Johnson observes in the Idler
no. 31, "pride has of all human vices the widest
dominion, appears in the greatest multiplicity of
forms, and lies hid under the greatest variety of
disguises" (Works, II, 95). Defined in his
Dictionary as an "inordinate and unreasonable
self-esteem," pride, he explains in one of his
sermons, is an "over-value set upon a man by himself"; it "mingles with all our other vices, and
without the most constant care, will mingle also
with our virtues."[12] Because of pride, Johnson
claims in the Rambler no. 21, "we are blinded in
examining our own labours by innumerable prejudices" (Works, III, 120). Here he argues that
"every man is prompted by the love of himself to
imagine, that he possesses some qualities, superior, either in kind or in degree, to those which
he sees allotted to the rest of the world; and,
whatever apparent disadvantages he may suffer in
the comparison with others, he has some invisible
distinctions, some latent reserve of excellence,
which he throws into the balance, and by which he
generally fancies that it is turned in his favour"
(Works, III, 115-16). "Vanity," defined in his
Dictionary as "arrogance" and "petty pride," generally "inclines us to find faults any where
rather than in ourselves" (Idler 70, Works, II,
218). Indeed, "the greatest human virtue," he
declares in the Rambler no. 104, "bears no proportion to human vanity. We always think ourselves better than we are, and are generally
desirous that others should think us still better
than we think ourselves" (Works, IV, 192). The
invariable human desires for fame, for wealth,
and for power, too, energetically expressed in
The Vanity of Human Wishes, are all products of
human pride and vanity.

Pride and vanity, thematically significant
throughout Jane Austen's comic-satiric fiction,
lie at the heart of her characterization in Pride
and Prejudice. The moralistic Mary Bennet ten-
dentiously explains these forms of self-deception
explored in the novel:

68

"Pride," observed Mary, who piqued
herself upon the solidity of her reflections, "is a very common failing I
believe. By all that I have ever read,
I am convinced that it is very common
indeed, that human nature is particularly prone to it, and that there are
very few of us who do not cherish a
feeling of self-complacency on the
score of some quality or other, real
or imaginary. Vanity and pride are
different things, though the words are
often used synonimously. A person may
be proud without being vain. Pride
relates more to our opinion of ourselves, vanity to what we would have
others think of us." (PP, 20)

An ironic turn on the pride of the speaker, whose
threadbare pieties are in fact a travesty of contemporary moral literature, this passage seriously
underscores Jane Austen's moral concern with the
major forms of self-deception. In Pride and
Prejudice Darcy, to whom readers commonly attribute the "Pride" in the title, is not the only one
who is early discovered "to be proud, to be above
his company, and above being pleased" (PP, 10).
Almost every other figure is characterized by the
inordinate degree to which he esteems himself or
wishes to be esteemed by others. Mr. Bingley's
sisters, for example, are "proud and conceited";
they believe they are "in every respect entitled
to think well of themselves, and meanly of others"
(PP, 15). Sir William Lucas, who has risen from
trade to the honors of knighthood, is proud of
his title. "The distinction," Jane Austen explains
with ironic restraint, "had perhaps been felt too
strongly" (PP, 18). Lydia Bennet, Elizabeth's
younger, soldier-hunting sister, has "a sort of
natural self-consequence, which the attention of
the officers . . . had increased into assurance"
(PP, 45). Mr. Collins is an odd "mixture of
pride and obsequiousness, self-importance and
humility" (PP, 70). Lady Catherine de Bourgh, his
patroness, is an "arrogant, conceited woman," full
of "affability and condescension" (PP, 84, 66).

69

And Miss Georgiana Darcy is believed for a long time to be, like her brother, "very, very proud" (PP, 82).

In this veritable maze of pride and hauteur, we may not easily recognize that Elizabeth Bennet, though acutely conscious of the pride around her, is herself a complex figure of "inordinate and unreasonable self-esteem." Intellectually proud, she deceives herself by confidently overestimating her ability to judge with ease and accuracy the character and behavior of others. To be sure, Elizabeth's power of judgment is, in many ways, as discriminating as her author's, and her rectitude is at times as penetrating and as unyielding as her author's. The marriage of her usually clearheaded, sensible friend Charlotte to the "conceited, pompous, narrow-minded, silly" Mr. Collins, for example, is to Elizabeth's mind both incomprehensible and indefensible (PP, 135). With similar clear sight she penetrates the veneer of superciliousness in Bingley's sisters, the impertinence of Lady Catherine, the rudeness and mean understanding of her mother Mrs. Bennet, the moral recklessness of her younger sisters, and the domestic irresponsibility of her father. But Elizabeth is deceiving herself when she invariably relies on her own discernment made on first impressions--to the exclusion of pertinent evidence. With "more quickness of observation" than her sister, who does not wish to be "hasty in censuring any one," Elizabeth seems absolutely stunned that Jane can "never see a fault in any body," that Jane can never "speak ill of a human being," that Jane can be "so honestly blind to the follies and nonsense of others" (PP, 14-15). What Elizabeth means, of course, is that she alone is not blind, that she alone can see accurately the faults of others.

Elizabeth's pride is often deftly masked by the excellence of her quick judgment; yet without injustice to her character, we may discriminate between the virtue and the fault. Elizabeth's week-long visit to Netherfield, as she nurses Jane back to good health, is the context of an

especially subtle dramatization of pride com-
mingling with keen intelligence. Mrs. Bennet,
at one point in Elizabeth's visit, awkwardly tries
to expedite the progress of Jane's romance by in-
sinuating to Bingley that he should on no account
think of leaving his estate "in a hurry" (PP, 42).
But Bingley demurs, acknowledging his characteristic haste. "Whatever I do," he says, "is done
in a hurry." Elizabeth suddenly declares that
this is "exactly" what she should have supposed
of him, and at Bingley's puzzlement in being so
easily comprehended, she readily adds: "Oh! yes--
I understand you perfectly." Perfect comprehension
of character on first impressions by this "studier
of character," as Bingley charmingly calls her,
would be a remarkable trait, were it only humanly
possible. Elizabeth, however, mistakenly believes
she possesses this power. Yet partly because the
conversation begins with a sufficiently valid
observation about Bingley, partly because it
gradually focuses on Mrs. Bennet's obnoxious hus-
band-hunting and her deliberate contempt for
Darcy, who gradually joins the conversation, and
partly because throughout this exchange we are
conscious of Elizabeth's acute awareness of the
intention and motivation of her mother, of Bingley
and of Darcy, we are likely to overlook the significance of Mrs. Bennet's reminder to Elizabeth
not to make hasty conclusions. Like Bingley,
Elizabeth is a victim of haste. She possesses a
valuable quickness of judgment, of which she is
all too perfectly assured.

That Elizabeth prizes her intelligence too
highly becomes increasingly clear by the following
evening when the Bingleys and their guests are all
gathered in the drawing room for conversation and
other diversion. Caroline Bingley coyly contends
for Darcy's attention by complimenting him on the
ease with which he writes letters to his sister.
In contrast to Darcy's style of writing, Bingley's
style is considered the "most careless way imag-
inable," and Bingley himself agrees that his
ideas "flow so rapidly" that he has not time to
express them, "by which means," he concludes, "my

letters sometimes convey no ideas at all to my correspondents" (PP, 48). Elizabeth, who has interestingly been silent throughout this discussion, suddenly intervenes, with some prejudice against Darcy, "Your humility, Mr. Bingley, must disarm reproof." By addressing Bingley in a manner which betrays approval of his precipitous way of thinking and writing, Elizabeth herself becomes subject to the same scrutiny with which Darcy analyzes his friend: "Nothing is more deceitful," Darcy says, "than the appearance of humility. It is . . . sometimes an indirect boast. . . . You are really proud of your defects in writing, because you consider them as proceeding from a rapidity of thought and carelessness of execution, which if not estimable, you think at least highly interesting." Darcy's observation really characterizes Elizabeth as much as it does Bingley. Elizabeth's facility is a "quickness of observation," and "The power of doing any thing with quickness," Darcy rightly maintains, "is always much prized by the possessor, and often without any attention to the imperfection of the performance" (PP, 49). Elizabeth will learn soon enough how mistaken her judgement about character and behavior may be. "I . . . have prided myself on my discernment," she will learn to say, "I . . . have valued myself on my abilities!" (PP, 208). Too highly.

While Elizabeth Bennet overvalues her power of judgment, Emma Woodhouse is prone to think too highly of her own social importance. But, unlike Elizabeth, who merely thinks more highly of her discernment than she ought, Emma vainly wishes others to recognize and defer to her superiority. "The real evils indeed of Emma's situation," Jane Austen announces with unerring succinctness, "were the power of having rather too much her own way, and a disposition to think a little too well of herself" (E, 5). The nature of Emma's deception is vanity, which Johnson's Dictionary defines as "petty pride" and "arrogance." She demands to be recognized as the successful planner of Miss Taylor and Mr. Weston's marriage, but Mr. Knightley pointedly asks her, "What are you proud of?--you made a lucky guess; and that is all that can be said" (E, 13). She perceives and patronizes Harriet Smith with similar vanity:

> . . . she found her altogether very en-
> gaging--not inconveniently shy, not
> unwilling to talk--and yet so far from
> pushing, shewing so proper and becoming
> a deference, seeming so pleasantly
> grateful for being admitted to Hartfield,
> and so artlessly impressed by the ap-
> pearance of every thing in so superior
> a style to what she had been used to,
> that she must have good sense and deserve
> encouragement. . . . She would notice
> her; she would improve her; she would
> detach her from her bad acquaintance,
> and introduce her into good society;
> she would form her opinions and her
> manners. It would be an interesting,
> and certainly a very kind undertaking;
> highly becoming her own situation in
> life, her leisure, and powers. (E, 23-24)

With clarity, grace and good humor, the passage explores the sophistry of a mind absorbed by its claims of social superiority. For what other purpose than the aggrandizement of Emma's impor-tance is Harriet "not inconveniently shy"? To whom other than Emma does Harriet show "so proper and becoming a deference"? Who other than Emma has "so superior a style" to Harriet that would justify her forming and improving the girl's opinions and manners?

Emma's vanity, of course, is not limited to the claims she makes on her former governess or on Harriet Smith; it extends the entire length and breadth of Highbury. The vain First Lady of Hartfield dissuades Harriet from seriously weighing Mr. Martin's proposal because she con-siders him a "very inferior creature" (E, 33). She deems Mr. Elton's surprising marriage pro-posal an example of blind "presumption in ad-dressing her" and of insupportable "arrogance" (E, 136). She vainly attaches more significance

73

to Churchill's attentions than is warranted. She condescendingly believes that the prosperous and friendly Coles family are "very respectable in their way," but that they "ought to be taught that it was not for them to arrange the terms on which the superior families would visit them" (E, 207). At their dinner party, "it suit/s/ Emma best to lead" at the piano; and, ironically, though she recognizes the mediocrity of her own performance and "never could attempt to conceal from herself" that Jane Fairfax's performance is "infinitely superior to her own," she is not unwilling to be praised more highly than she deserves (E, 227). Emma, who is "so truly beloved and important; so always first and always right" (E, 84) in her father's eyes, is in fact "never loth to be first" in anyone else's (E, 71). "I always deserve the best treatment," she pertly tells Knightley, "because I never put up with any other" (E, 474). And though she may not realize it at the time, she is really speaking of herself when she observes, "Where little minds belong to rich people in authority, I think they have a knack of swelling out, till they are quite as unmanageable as great ones" (E, 147). For a long time, Emma is a fully deceived snob, who amply justifies Dr. Johnson's observation that "We always think ourselves better than we are, and are generally desirous that others should think us still better than we think ourselves" (Rambler 104, Works, IV, 192). But Emma's story will not close before she discovers and regrets her "insufferable vanity" and her "unpardonable arrogance" (E, 412, 413).

Emma Woodhouse and Elizabeth Bennet convincingly represent not only forms of self-deception discussed theoretically in Johnson's essays, they also dramatically validate the Johnsonian conviction that self-deception often leads to serious consequences. Fully aware of the grim outcome to which self-deception could lead, Johnson warns in his Life of Savage that "the danger of this pleasing intoxication must not be concealed," for Savage, "by imputing none of his miseries to himself . . . continued to act upon the same principles, and to follow the same path" and "was

never made wiser by his sufferings, nor preserved
by one misfortune from falling into another"
(Lives, II, 380). Such serious moral language
may seem remote from the spirited worlds of Emma
and Pride and Prejudice, but the tenor of
Johnson's remarks is entirely appropriate to Emma's
and to Elizabeth's character and situation. Both
heroines, like the self-deceivers in Johnson's
Rambler no. 31, comically "weave their sophistry
till their own reason is entangled" and both,
until they discover the source of their deception,
tread--like Richard Savage--"the same steps on the
same circle" (Works, III, 173).

Invariably more self aware than Emma,
Elizabeth nonetheless has a pride which is poten-
tially as menacing as Emma's. The clearest moral
consequence of Elizabeth's pride is her lack of
candor. "Candour" does not mean today what it
signified in the eighteenth century. It did not
mean "honesty in expressing oneself" or "frankness."
Rather, as defined in Johnson's Dictionary, it
signified "sweetness of temper; kindness"; its
cognate "candid" meant "free from malice, not
desirous to find faults." "Candour" is defined
for us also by Elizabeth, when she compliments her
sister Jane for discounting malicious rumors about
others, for her ability "to be candid without os-
tentation or design--to take the good of every
body's character and make it still better, and
say nothing of the bad" (PP, 14). Unlike Jane,
who does not wish to be "hasty in censuring anyone," Elizabeth seems positively bent on censuring
someone. The conflicting stories of Darcy and
Wickham leave Jane only with uncertainties and
questions. She finds it so "difficult" and "distressing" that she does not know what to think
(PP, 80). Blindly censuring Darcy for his pride,
Elizabeth resolves against "attention, forbearance,
patience," and turns away from him at their next
encounter "with a degree of ill humour" (PP, 89).
At Charlotte's suggestion that Elizabeth might
find Darcy "very agreeable," she impetuously pro-
tests, "Heaven forbid!--That would be the greatest
misfortune of all!--To find a man agreeable whom

75

one is determined to hate!--Do not wish me such
an evil" (PP, 90).

Elizabeth's pride is a constant temptation
to speak without candor, and all her charm and
wit cannot conceal the bitterness and faultfinding
with which she occasionally yields to it. Dis-
tressed by Jane's disappointment at Bingley's
unexpected departure and by Charlotte's mercenary
marriage to Mr. Collins, she angrily confides in
her sister: "There are few people whom I really
love, and still fewer of whom I think well. The
more I see of the world, the more I am dissatisfied
with it; and every day confirms my belief of the
inconsistency of all human characters, and of the
little dependence that can be placed on the appearance of either merit or sense" (PP, 135). Too
conscious of the shortcomings of others and unaware
of her own erroneous prejudices and her own fal-
lible judgment, Elizabeth tacitly excludes herself
from the weaknesses of human nature. When intro-
duced to Miss Anne de Bourgh, she bitterly tells
herself, "I like her appearance; she looks sickly
and cross" (PP, 158). When informed of Wickham's
interlude with Mary King, she believes "he never
cared three straws about . . . . such a nasty
little freckled thing" (PP, 220). And when in
London with her aunt Mrs. Gardiner, she bitterly
rails against Darcy, Wickham, Bingley, and Collins
altogether: "I have a very poor opinion of young
men who live in Derbyshire; and their intimate
friends who live in Hertfordshire are not much
better. I am sick of them all. Thank Heaven! I
am going tomorrow where I shall find a man who
has not one agreeable quality . . . to recommend
him. Stupid men are the only ones worth knowing,
after all" (PP, 154). But "the misfortune of
speaking with bitterness," Elizabeth will soon
learn to acknowledge, "is a most natural consequence of the prejudices /she7 had been encouraging"
(PP, 226). She will soon be sorry for "every
saucy speech" she had ever directed towards Darcy
and for every act of "impertinence" (PP, 380).
Most of all, she will heartily regret the "petulance and acrimony" with which she refuses his
proposal of marriage (PP, 265).

If Elizabeth's pride impels her to speak
without candor and occasionally with petulance
and acrimony, Emma's pride leads to more serious
consequences. Something of a casuist, Emma
effortlessly rationalizes Frank Churchill's puz-
zling sixteen-mile trip to London for the single
purpose of having his hair cut.[13] "I do not know
whether it ought to be so," she informs a reproach-
ful Mr. Knightley, "but certainly silly things do
cease to be silly if they are done by sensible
people in an impudent way. Wickedness is always
wickedness, but folly is not always folly" (E,
212). Though amused by the convenient sophistry
with which Emma deceives herself, we are nonetheless aware of the grim consequences to which such
self-deception may lead. "Every one sees the
folly of . . . mean doublings to escape the per-
suit of criticism," Johnson observes in the
Rambler no. 31, which examines the culpability of
defending known mistakes (Works, III, 171). "It
is happy," he adds, "when this temper discovers
itself only in little things, which may be right
or wrong without any influence on the virtue or
happiness of mankind." Unfortunately Emma indulges her pride on issues far more important than
Frank's haircut. With uncommon casuistry she
undertakes the most officious manipulation of
Harriet's life, justifying herself against the
rational arguments of Mr. Knightley, who warns
her: "Better be without sense, than misapply it
as you do" (E, 64). Mr. Elton's abrupt and unexpected proposal of marriage helps Emma recognize
that "It was foolish, . . . wrong, to take so
active a part in bringing any two people together . . . . adventuring too far, assuming too
much, making light of what ought to be serious,
a trick of what ought to be simple," yet we soon
find her reasoning herself back into matchmaking
(E, 136-37).

Less amusing than her intrusions into
Harriet's life are Emma's inexcusable suspicions
of Jane Fairfax. Though in part misled by Frank
Churchill's deliberate deceptions--as Elizabeth
is misled by Wickham's--Emma is guilty, like
Elizabeth, of judging without candor. On the

flimsy basis of Jane's not going to Ireland with the Campbells and of Jane's being "so cold, so cautious," so "suspiciously reserved," Emma unkindly concludes that she must have an adulterous relationship with Mr. Dixon (E, 169). Although Jane is not a fully drawn personality, we know enough about her to recognize the psychological duress she is living under. Soon to make her way alone in the world as a governess, she all the while patiently endures the officious and condescending attention of Mrs. Augusta Elton, whose attempts to manipulate her represent the dark side of Emma's manipulation of Harriet. We can sense some of the pain Jane suffers when John Knightley inadvertently brings tears to her eyes as he reminds her of the situation she is about to face. How much more distress do Churchill's tricks at Emma's encouragement cause? Jane's perceptible blushes, her occasionally angry responses, and her uneasy laughter, as well as her steady refusal to be comforted by Emma during her illness, only suggest the amount of pain Emma's vain behavior leads to.

More serious than either her manipulation of Harriet or her unkind suspicions of Jane is the cruel insensitivity Emma shows to a lifelong friend of the family, Miss Bates. It is particularly tragic that Emma is unable to resist the temptation to insult the elderly and impecunious daughter of the former vicar. Emma's insensitive comment to Miss Bates at the Box Hill picnic assumes grave dimensions even within this comic novel, because though speaking in the immediate context of Churchill's game playing, she violates the innocent childlikeness with which Miss Bates proposes to cooperate in the general merriment. "Looking round with the most good-humoured dependence on every body's assent," Miss Bates confesses to the gathered picknickers that she will be sure to say "three things very dull indeed" as soon as she opens her mouth (E, 370). Cruelly taking advantage of the vulnerable woman's position, Emma politely reminds her: "Ah! ma'am, but there may be a difficulty. Pardon me--but you will be limited as to number--only three at once." Miss

Bates is deceived at first by the "mock ceremony" of Emma's manner, but when Emma's meaning finally bursts upon her, "a slight blush showed that it could pain her" (E, 371). Emma has violated the moral principle of compassion, and Mr. Knightley sternly reproaches her for the gravity of her offense, reminding her of Miss Bates's poverty and old age. A moment's reflection on the "pride of the moment" (375) is all that is necessary for Emma to realize she has been "so brutal, so cruel to Miss Bates!" (E, 376).

If we pause to examine the sources of Emma's and Elizabeth's self-deception, we may notice some striking correspondences between Jane Austen's delineation of character and Samuel Johnson's reflections on the causes of deception. Self-deception, Johnson emphasizes, is pleasant because it provides an alternative to the truth, which is generally disagreeable and "contrary to our wishes and opposite to our practice" (Rambler 96, Works, IV, 149). Self-knowledge, therefore, becomes increasingly difficult, because "as our attention naturally follows our interest, we hear unwillingly what we are afraid to know, and soon forget what we have no inclination to impress upon our memories."

The convenient disposition to attend only to what is pleasing, while suppressing everything which makes us uncomfortable, leads to a second major source of self-deception, flattery. Because "men are willing to credit what they wish," Johnson says, they "encourage rather those who gratify them with pleasure, than those that instruct them with fidelity" (Idler 20, Works, II, 62). "No man," he observes elsewhere, "is much pleased with a companion, who does not encrease, in some respect, his fondness of himself" (Rambler 104, Works, IV, 191). A person will naturally encourage and take pleasure in those who flatter him; conversely, unwillingness to believe what he does not wish to hear will permit him to find excuses for being undisturbed by unpleasant accusations. A person may deceive himself, finally, because he is unaware of the motives of his judgments and actions. "We are sometimes not ourselves conscious of the original motives of our actions," Johnson notes in the Rambler no. 87 (Works, IV, 95).

For all her keen perception of character, Elizabeth Bennet is singularly unaware that her prejudice towards Darcy is rooted in her wounded pride. Before they have ever met, Darcy has humiliated her to Bingley by saying, "She is tolerable; but not handsome enough to tempt me" (PP, 12). Elizabeth may spiritedly relate this story to all her friends, but the incident is sufficiently painful to leave her with "no very cordial feelings towards him." Though she readily acknowledges to Charlotte Lucas--"I could easily forgive his pride, if he had not mortified mine"-- she is curiously unaware that the unpleasant truth ("she is not half so handsome as Jane," Mrs. Bennet says) has inclined her to seek pleasure in offending Darcy (PP, 20). "I meant to be uncommonly clever in taking so decided a dislike to him, without any reason," she informs her sister Jane. "It is such a spur to one's genius, such an opening for wit to have a dislike of that kind" (PP, 226). And Elizabeth has never lacked the flattery of her family and friends, who all confide in her. But Elizabeth's convenient disposition to attend only to what is pleasant and to be flattered by the encouragement of her friends does not account for the unconscious motives that have contributed to her self-deception. Elizabeth is predisposed to believing Wickham's slanderous rumors and innuendoes about Darcy largely because she is unwittingly growing attracted to Wickham. The desire to be pleased, the flattery of her friends, and her unconscious attraction to Wickham, then, all render Elizabeth partially blind.

Although we may piece together only fragmentarily the sources of Elizabeth's self-deception, we can see how thoroughly Jane Austen considers the sources of Emma's self-deceit. Somewhat like Elizabeth, Emma is spoiled by her "affectionate, indulgent" father (E, 5). Undisciplined by her

gentle and uncritical governess, Emma grows to
derive enormous pleasure from her vain and childish
undertakings for other people. She vainly looks
upon her undertakings "with the real good-will of
a mind delighted with its own ideas" (E, 24).

The pleasure Emma derives from patronizingly
arranging other people's lives is augmented by
the flattery of her friends. Mr. Elton weak-
mindedly compliments her on her "improvement" of
Harriet, and vacuously encourages and flatters
her talent for drawing. Frank Churchill, too,
performs his share of flattery, which Emma is not
at all likely to reject. Even Mr. Knightley, who
"never flatter/s/" (11) her but who knows she is
"anxious for a compliment" regarding Harriet,
reluctantly concedes, "She really does you credit"
(E, 58). But Knightley is perfectly aware that
Harriet, who "knows nothing herself, and looks
upon Emma as knowing every thing," is an undesigning
"flatterer in all her ways" (E, 38). With apparent artlessness, Harriet privately assures Emma:
"Nobody is equal to you!" (E, 268).

Jane Austen explores in Pride and Prejudice
and Emma the forms, causes, and consequences of
her heroines' self-deception only to show how by
degrees they learn that "most valuable knowledge"
necessary for their happiness and fulfillment.
The means by which Elizabeth and Emma acquire this
self-knowledge reflect, in a variety of ways, the
practical methods Samuel Johnson suggests in his
essays. Simply recognizing the sources of self-
deception, Johnson believed, is the most significant step towards their elimination. "However we
may labour for our own deception," he remarks in
the Idler no. 80, "truth, though unwelcome, will
sometimes intrude upon the mind" (Works, II, 250).
It is necessary to encourage this "intrusion" of
truth, he adds, by recollecting whatever is unpleasing to us and by cultivating an awareness of
our motives of behavior. Johnson, therefore,
emphasizes the importance of regular self-
examination. He suggests, in the Rambler no. 155,
that "it might perhaps be useful to the conquest

of all these ensnarers of the mind, if at certain
stated days life was reviewed" (Works, V, 65).
In the Rambler no. 28, he carefully discusses the
necessity of "assigning proper portions of . . .
life to the examination of the rest" (Works, III,
156). Another significant method of achieving
self-knowledge is what Johnson quaintly calls the
"frequent consultation of a wise friend, admitted
to intimacy, and encouraged to sincerity" (Works,
III, 154). The advantage of such a relationship
is that a friend may point out the failings which
escape our own notice, for "friendship without
/sincerity/ is of a very little value; since the
great use of so close an intimacy is that our
virtues may be guarded and encouraged, and our
vices repressed in their first appearance by
timely detection, and salutary remonstrances"
(Rambler 40, Works, III, 220). Those friends who
can and do penetrate the hidden springs of our
conduct may call our attention to those aspects
of our behavior which are inherently self-deceptive.

     Elizabeth Bennet discovers the source of her
self-deception only after regular reflection,
scrupulous inquiry, and systematic self-examination.
She often searches for the truth alone and with
the thoroughness of a trained analyst. Again and
again we find her in solitude, pondering, wondering,   examining, and re-examining the meaning of
conduct and motives. With juridical attention,
for example, Elizabeth examines the letter which
Darcy hopes will explain his behavior. At first,
of course, she reads it with a "strong prejudice"
against Darcy, with an "eagerness" which leaves
her little power of comprehension, and with such
an "impatience" that she is "incapable of attending to the sense . . . before her eyes" (PP,
204). Darcy's assumption about Jane's coolness
towards Bingley she "instantly resolved to be
false," and his account of the family obstacles
to the match makes her "too angry to have any
wish of doing him justice." When she more attentively reads the account concerning Wickham, her
feelings are "more acutely painful and more difficult of definition." Johnson reminds us that

"truth is, indeed, not often welcome for its own
sake; it is generally unpleasing because contrary
to our wishes and opposite to our practice"
(Rambler 96, Works, IV, 149). We recall how painful it would have been for Elizabeth to discover
earlier the falsity of her accusations against
Darcy, how much more difficult it would have been
to accept Caroline Bingley's testimony that
Wickham's story was "perfectly false," and how
much pleasanter it was to accept the deceptions
of this charming slanderer (PP, 204). Now, as
Elizabeth peruses Darcy's letter, the same inclination to disbelieve everything seizes her. "This
must be false!" she exclaims to herself. "This
cannot be! This must be the grossest falsehood!"
But, as Johnson observes with psychological acuity,
"However we may labour for our own deception,
truth, though unwelcome, will sometimes intrude
upon the mind" (Idler 80, Works, II, 250). With
a "perturbed state of mind" and "with thoughts
that could rest on nothing," therefore, Elizabeth
walks on (PP, 205). Within minutes, she again
pores over the letter, commanding herself "to
examine the meaning of every sentence." She
momentarily puts the letter down and "weigh/s/
every circumstance" and "deliberate/s/ on the
probability of each statement." Remembering that
she has never wished to inquire about Wickham's
real character, she desperately tries "to recol-
lect" some instance of Wickham's goodness, but "no
such recollection befriend/s/ her." Elizabeth
realizes that though Wickham has lied to her in
several instances, she had been predisposed to
believing him without question. At length discovering the truth, that she has been "blind,
partial, prejudiced, absurd," Elizabeth exclaims
to herself:

How despicably have I acted! . . .
I, who have prided myself on my discernment!--I, who have valued myself on my
abilities! who have often disdained the
generous candour of my sister, and gratified my vanity, in useless or blameable
distrust.--How humiliating is this
discovery!--Yet, how just a humiliation!--

> Had I been in love, I could not have
> been more wretchedly blind. But vanity,
> not love, has been my folly. (PP, 208)

The passage represents a climactic moment in
Elizabeth's moral development; it truly marks for
her the dawning of self-knowledge. But it is
only the dawn, for the central irony of Elizabeth's
reflection is that, while she fully recognizes the
pride in her self-deception, there remain some
corners of her mind and heart yet unknown to her.
"Had I been in love," Elizabeth says. Even in her
humiliating and wretched frame of mind, Elizabeth
makes us laugh, because we know that she already
has begun to fall in love with Darcy.

In the third and final volume of Pride and
Prejudice, then, Jane Austen explores the process
by which Elizabeth discovers this knowledge. In
the midst of other people Elizabeth cannot think
clearly; she reserves for solitude "the delight
of unpleasant recollections" (PP, 212). When she
reads Darcy's letter again, "her anger" is "turned
against herself." At Pemberley, after listening
intently to Mrs. Reynolds' unqualified praise of
her employer, she stands thoughtfully and sympathetically before his portrait; and that night,
a transition begins to take place in her mind:

> The respect created by the conviction of
> his valuable qualities, though at first
> unwillingly admitted, had for some time
> ceased to be repugnant to her feelings;
> and it was now heightened into somewhat
> of a friendlier nature, by the testimony
> so highly in his favour, and bringing
> forward his disposition in so amiable
> a light, which yesterday had produced.
> But above all, above respect and esteem,
> there was a motive within her of good
> will which could not be overlooked. It
> was gratitude. . . . She respected, she
> esteemed, she was grateful to him, she
> felt a real interest in his welfare;
> and she only wanted to know how far she
> wished that welfare to depend upon her-

self, and how far it would be for the
happiness of both that she should employ
the power, which her fancy told her she
still possessed, of bringing on the re-
newal of his addresses. (PP, 265-66)

Jane Austen flawlessly records in this representation of Elizabeth's thoughts and feelings a remarkably graceful transition from respect and
esteem to gratitude and love. The respect which
"heightened into somewhat of a friendlier nature"
is a felicitous phrase denoting the durable foundation for their real mutual affection.

Elizabeth gradually begins to comprehend that
Darcy is "exactly the man, who, in disposition
and talents, would most suit her" (PP, 312). Their
marriage, she finally acknowledges, is a "union
that must have been to the advantage of both";
her "ease and liveliness" must be a perfect complement to his "judgment, information, and knowledge." "He is a gentleman," Elizabeth pertly
informs the officious Lady Catherine, "I am a
gentleman's daughter; so far we are equal" (PP,
356). But Elizabeth's flippancy misrepresents
the essential truth of her assertion. She and
Darcy are equal in affection and virtue--and in
that "most valuable knowledge" of themselves.
Their mutual confession of love makes clear that
they have each contributed to the enlightenment
of the other. Elizabeth acknowledges the part his
letter had in destroying all her former prejudices.
Darcy, in turn, acknowledges her part in the
gradual diminution of his pride. Secure in the
knowledge of themselves and in their affection
for each other, their perfect marriage is more
than a social occasion, it is a moral celebration.

Like Elizabeth, Emma Woodhouse discovers
that "most valuable knowledge" of herself both
through self-examination and, almost as important,
through the concern and guidance of her dearest
friend Mr. Knightley. Periodical reflection--
often the locus of moral backsliding in the comic
world of Emma--is the primary means by which Emma
discovers the source of her vanity. Mr. Knightley's

85

warning to Emma about the ill consequences of
persuading Harriet to reject Martin prompts her
to examine herself: "She did not always feel
so absolutely satisfied with herself, so entirely
convinced that her opinions were right and her
adversary's wrong, as Mr. Knightley" (E, 67).
But within moments, she is able to satisfy her
conscience by surmising that Knightley could not
possibly have "the skill of such an observer on
such a question as herself." Convinced that
Knightley has spoken "hastily and in anger," she
believes "he had rather said what he wished re-
sentfully to be true, than what he knew any thing
about." In effect, Jane Austen amusingly tells
us, though Knightley can quarrel with her, "Emma
could not quarrel with herself" (E, 69). Though
much of Emma's reflection and occasional remorse
resounds with rich comic irony, there is still a
good deal of effectiveness to the practice. Emma
does learn to see her faults. After renewed
examination, she realizes that she has acted with
as much vanity towards Jane Fairfax as towards
Harriet Smith. And for insulting the elderly
Miss Bates Emma is completely repentant. The
sudden painful recognition of her malice towards
the vulnerable woman fully repels her: "She was
vexed beyond what could have been expressed--
almost beyond what she could conceal. Never had
she felt so agitated, mortified, grieved, at any
circumstance in her life. She was most forcibly
struck" (E, 376).

     Almost as important as reflection in Emma's
moral awakening is the concern and guidance of
her dearest friend Mr. Knightley. Only Mr.
Knightley, described by the author as a "sensible
man" and as a "very old and intimate friend of the
family," enjoys an amiable, unconstrained and
instructive relationship with Emma (E, 9).
Knightley and Emma can talk freely together, too,
for as Emma says, "We always say what we like to
one another" (E, 10). Though he "love/s/ her
really too well to be unjust or unkind," Knightley's
"very sincere interest" in Emma makes him unwilling
to compromise principle or to refrain from just

criticism (E, 40). They may strongly disagree
over Harriet, for example, but they soon "become
friends again"; and although their reconciliation
begins with Knightley's "grave looks and short
questions," they gradually talk more openly and
intimately as Knightley quietly takes Emma's
niece from her arms "with all the unceremoniousness
of perfect amity" (E, 98). Knightley is for Emma
the perfect embodiment of the Johnsonian friend
and mentor--the "wise friend, admitted to intimacy,
and encouraged to sincerity" (Rambler 28, Works,
III, 154).

    Knightley teaches Emma and reminds her of
her failings; that is for Emma the chief benefit
of their sincere and long-standing friendship.
In characterizing Knightley, Jane Austen vitalizes
Johnson's notion that "friendship without /sin-
cerity/ is of a very little value" (Rambler 40,
Works, III, 220). Throughout their long and intimate relationship Knightley admonishes Emma,
but nowhere more severely than when Emma's vanity
leads to her cruel insensitivity to Miss Bates.
The reproof is strong, but it comes from a sincere
and concerned friend: "This is not pleasant to
you, Emma--and it is very far from pleasant to me;
but I must, I will,--I will tell you truths while
I can, satisfied with proving myself your friend
by very faithful counsel, and trusting that you
will some time or other do me greater justice
than you can do now" (E, 375). Even at the moment
of confessing his love for her, Knightley reminds
Emma of his sincere friendship: "You hear nothing
but truth from me.--I have blamed you, and lectured
you, and you have borne it as no other woman in
England would have borne it" (E, 430).

    The most beautiful aspect of Emma is that
the process of Emma's moral development is co-
extensive with the growth of her attachment and
love for Knightley. From the beginning we are
satisfactorily aware that the lasting friendship
between Emma and Knightley will eventually lead
to marriage. The only question is when Emma will
recognize this. Ironically, Emma begins to recognize the kind of friendship she shares with

87

Knightley when--vanity abounding--Emma's taking
second place to Mrs. Elton at the Crown Inn dance
is "almost enough to make her think of marrying"
(E, 325). Finally accepting Knightley's most
pleasant invitation to dance, Emma reminds him,
"You know we are not really so much brother and
sister as to make it at all improper." "Brother
and sister! no, indeed," Knightley exclaims (E,
331). Characteristically, Knightley's proposal
is the climax of a long and steady, affectionate
friendship. Emma and he are walking reflectively--
she still under the assumption that he must be in
love with Harriet, Knightley under the assumption
that she is still in love with Churchill. Emma
at first persuades him to stop when she painfully
believes he is on the verge of confiding his love
for Harriet, but then retracts. "I stopped you
ungraciously, just now, Mr. Knightley," she says,
"and, I am afraid, gave you pain." She entreats
him, "If you have any wish to speak openly to me
as a friend, or to ask my opinion of any thing
that you may have in contemplation--as a friend,
indeed, you may command me.--I will hear whatever
you like. I will tell you exactly what I think."
"As a friend!" Knightley nearly gasps, but then
recovers and replies, "Extraordinary as it may
seem, I accept it, and refer myself to you as a
friend. . . . God knows, I have been a very in-
different lover" (E, 429-30).

Knightley and Emma therefore perfectly deserve their marriage, which in Dr. Johnson's
language is "the strictest tye of perpetual
friendship" (Rambler 18, Works, III, 103), or (in
the words of his fictitious correspondents
Hymenaeus and Tranquilla) "the most solemn league
of perpetual friendship, a state from which arti-
fice and concealment are to be banished for ever,
and in which every act of dissimulation is a
breach of faith" (Rambler 167, Works, V, 124).
Their marriage has triumphantly issued from a long
and true friendship. As Elizabeth Bennet's pliant
and lively temper will soften Darcy's rigidity,
Emma's vivacity will be a salutary complement to
Knightley's restraint. Knightley assures Emma

that they have "every right that equal worth can give, to be happy together" (E, 465). Mrs. Weston is convinced of their "equal importance," and Mr. Weston is equally certain their marriage is "all right, all open, all equal" (E, 468). Thus, Emma and Knightley marry symbolically amidst a "small band of true friends" who witness the ceremony, and all their hopes, confidence, and predictions are fulfilled in the "perfect happiness of the union" (E, 484). Emma's self-knowledge is celebrated in marriage.

No perfunctory conclusion to the story of a vain social manipulator, as some critics mistakenly assume, marriage represents a real change in the life of this maturing young woman. Emma Woodhouse, like Elizabeth Bennet, has come to recognize the form of pride by which she has deceived herself and by which she has courted serious moral error. Both heroines, through habitual reflection and self-examination and even the vigilant guidance of a sympathetic friend, have uncovered in moments of rich comic irony the sources of their deception, and both have achieved that "most valuable knowledge" which permits them to fulfill their known responsibilities in life. By tracing in their lives the recognizably eighteenth-century pattern of moral growth and by identifying Jane Austen's demonstrably Johnsonian methods of detecting and avoiding self-deception, we as readers can understand fully why marriage is a fitting conclusion to their acquired self-knowledge. Elizabeth and Emma, secure in the knowledge of themselves, deserve to be happy.

Emma's and Elizabeth's discovery of the common vanity and pride by which they have been deceived and their achievement of self-knowledge are morally prerequisite to their happiness in marriage. In Jane Austen's last work, Persuasion, the heroine Anne Elliot is at the beginning of the novel perfectly self-aware and secure in the knowledge of herself and of her duty. In this novel Jane Austen dramatically explores the intensity of feeling which vitalizes her heroine's Johnsonian sense of principle, and which unites her morally with all the heroines who precede her, especially with Elinor Dashwood, of whom she seems a successful re-creation. The consistency of Jane Austen's moral vision throughout her writing career makes Persuasion an appropriate novel on which to conclude.

NOTES

[1]G. B. Stern and Sheila Kaye-Smith, Talking of Jane Austen (New York: Harper, 1944), p. 176.

[2]H. W. Garrod, "Jane Austen: A Depreciation," Essays by Divers Hands: Transactions of the Royal Society of Literature, n. s., 8 (1928), 36.

[3]Mark Schorer, "The Humiliation of Emma Woodhouse," in Ian Watt, ed., Jane Austen: A Collection of Critical Essays (Englewood Cliffs, N. J.: Prentice-Hall, 1963), p. 109.

[4]Edmund Wilson, "A Long Talk about Jane Austen," in Ian Watt, ed., Jane Austen: A Collection of Critical Essays, p. 39.

[5]Marvin Mudrick, Jane Austen: Irony as Defense and Discovery (1952; rpt. Berkeley: University of California Press, 1968), p. 206.

[6]Mudrick, p. 124.

[7]Garrod, p. 36.

[8]Mark Schorer, "Introduction" to Pride and Prejudice (Boston: Houghton Mifflin, 1956), p. xii.

[9]For the reference to Emma see James Edward Austen-Leigh, Memoir of Jane Austen, ed. R. W. Chapman (1926; rpt. Oxford: Clarendon Press, 1967), p. 157.

[10]For a systematic discussion of Johnson's views on self-deception see Paul Kent Alkon, Samuel Johnson and Moral Discipline (Chicago: Northwestern Univ. Press, 1967), pp. 109-145.

[11]See Kenneth L. Moler, Jane Austen's Art of Allusion (Lincoln: Univ. of Nebraska Press, 1968), pp. 2-10.

91

[12]Sermon VI, The Works of Samuel Johnson, LL.D. (1787; rpt. Oxford: Oxford Univ. Press, 1825), IX, 343.

[13]That Frank Churchill travels to London primarily to purchase the pianoforte for Jane Fairfax in secret does not alter the effect of Emma's rationalization.

CHAPTER V

EXPLORATION OF FEELING IN SENSE AND SENSIBILITY
AND PERSUASION

Sense and Sensibility and Persuasion stand
not only at opposite ends of Jane Austen's writing
career, but, according to several contemporary
critics, at thematically contradictory poles as
well. Marvin Mudrick satisfactorily distinguishes
the seemingly conflicting themes: although Jane
Austen intends to parody excessive feeling in
Sense and Sensibility, she in fact shows that
"not merely false feeling, but feeling itself, is
bad" and that "the only cure for a passionate
heart is to remove it"; Persuasion, on the other
hand, has "a new impulse, feeling; and a new
climax, self-fulfillment."[1] Even those who would
disagree with Mudrick's claims point to the
uniqueness of Persuasion in Jane Austen's works.
A. Walton Litz, for example, locates one of its
unique attributes in the heroine, Anne Elliot,
who is "locked in the world of her own consciousness" and whose "despair is that of the modern
'personality' forced to live within itself."[2]
Howard Babb similarly argues that the novel vindicates completely what can only be called Anne
Elliot's major intuitions, . . . that is, a mode
of apprehension essentially emotional and in-
tensely subjective."[3] There is, however, much
less dissimilarity between Persuasion and the rest
of Jane Austen's novels, Sense and Sensibility in
particular, than these interpretations suggest.
In fact, it would be truer to say that her last
novel is an artistically successful exploration
of the same theme which the earlier novel narrow-
ly and unrealistically explores--the subordination
of feeling to reason and moral principle.

Walton Litz pointedly suggests why, in han-
dling the respective merits of reason and feeling
in Sense and Sensibility, Jane Austen appears to
offer no convincing integration of the two attributes, but only an exaggerated defense of reason.

and an unqualified attack on all feeling. "Jane
Austen," he surmises, "was working against her
natural inclinations and talents. She was the
victim of conventions, but these were primarily
artistic, not social."[4] Doubtless correct as far
as it goes, such conjecture acknowledges neither
the moral norms represented in this novel nor
their source, the work of familiar eighteenth-
century moralists like Samuel Johnson.

A characteristic scene from Sense and
Sensibility may suggest the degree to which a
rigid moral structure dominates--and ultimately
weakens--the dramatic effectiveness of the novel
and its characters. In what appears to be a deliberate breach of social propriety, Marianne
Dashwood travels to the estate of Mrs. Smith in
Allenham with no other escort than her recent acquaintance, Mr. Willoughby, and later informs
Elinor that she never spent a more pleasant morning
in her life. While Elinor gravely reminds her
sister that "the pleasantness of an employment
does not always evince its propriety," Marianne
emotionally replies, "On the contrary, nothing can
be a stronger proof of it, Elinor; for if there
had been any real impropriety in what I did, I
should have been sensible of it at the time, for
we always know when we are acting wrong, and with
such a conviction I could have had no pleasure"
(SS, 68). The tone of Elinor's reprimand makes
clear that moral, as well as social, propriety
cannot be determined by instinctive feeling. This
principle, which Jane Austen conveys in all her
novels, is implied in Mansfield Park, for example,
when the author describes the long-standing, affectionate relationship between Fanny Price and
her brother William, and soberly observes that
such relationships do not invariably exist, that
because of the unreliability of instinctive feeling
the early affection of brother and sister may over
a period of time erode and eventually be severed:
"Too often, alas! it is so.--Fraternal love, some
times almost every thing, is at others worse than
nothing" (MP, 235). In the same novel, Fanny's
return to her natural mother in Portsmouth is

marked by no uncommon severance of natural affections: "Mrs. Price was not unkind--but, instead
of gaining on her affection and confidence, and
becoming more and more dear, her daughter never
met with greater kindness from her, than on the
first day of her arrival. The instinct of nature
was soon satisfied, and Mrs. Price's attachment
had no other source" (MP, 389). In Persuasion,
too, Elizabeth Elliot's natural affection for her
sister Anne is severed and replaced by a spurious
friendship with the designing Mrs. Clay.
Elizabeth's conduct is seen disapprovingly by
Lady Russell--and implicitly by Jane Austen--as
a "turning from the society of so deserving a
sister to bestow her affection and confidence on
one who ought to have been nothing to her but the
object of distant civility" (P, 16).

Moral conduct, these examples demonstrate,
cannot be determined by natural affection or,
indeed, by any instinctive feeling. They demonstrate, too, that Jane Austen differed significantly from moral philosophers like Francis
Hutcheson and Lord Shaftesbury, who argued that
man is naturally benevolent, that he has an innate
moral sense which spontaneously leads him to satisfy impulses of sympathetic good will in personal
relationships. "The notions and principles of
fair, just and honest, with the rest of these
ideas, are innate," Shaftesbury maintains in his
Characteristics of Men, Manners, Opinions, Times
(1711); and "instinct," which he later substitutes
for "innate," is "that which Nature teaches us,
exclusive of art, culture, or discipline."[5] The
principal theorist behind Marianne Dashwood's
personal moral philosophy, Lord Shaftesbury,
argues that "no creature can do ill without being
conscious of his offense and without having a
feeling of deserved punishment."[6] Applied in
full--as Marianne would like--Shaftesbury's doctrine of an innate moral sense would make the
moral norm a variable rather than a constant
standard; since individuals differ from each other,
and likewise have within themselves, at various
times, instinctual feelings that are widely dis-

similar. Were moral conduct dependent wholly on
feelings, or on passing intuitions, were instinctual reactions as reliable as studied judgments,
the need for rational and moral restraint would
be unnecessary.

Samuel Johnson (and Jane Austen after him)
clearly saw these implications in Shaftesbury's
moral theory, and on innumerable occasions refuted
or ridiculed them. The "wise philosopher" in
Rasselas, for example, who advises the prince "to
live according to nature, in obedience to that
universal and unalterable law, with which every
heart is originally impressed; which is not written on it by precept, but graven by destiny, not
instilled by education, but infused at our nativ-
ity," is soon found to be "one of the sages whom
he should understand less, as he heard him longer"
(R, xxii, 98). Throughout his life, in fact,
Johnson energetically refuted the Shaftesburian
notion that moral conduct is a matter of feeling
rather than a function of reason informed by principle. Johnson's celebrated strictures on
Fielding, founded on his objection to conduct
guided by spontaneous moral feeling, are summa-
rized by his early biographer Sir John Hawkins:
"/Fielding's/ morality, in respect that it resolves virtue into good affections, in contradiction to moral obligation and a sense of duty, is
that of Lord Shaftesbury vulgarized, and is a
system of excellent use in palliating the vices
most injurious to society. He was the inventor
of that cant-phrase, goodness of heart, which is
every day used as a substitute for probity, and
means little more than the virtue of a horse or
dog."[7]

With the same intellectual vigor, Johnson
denied the popular belief that men are endowed
with instinctive affection for their immediate
relations. "I believe natural affection, of
which we hear so much, is very small," Boswell
once suggested to him; but Johnson retorted, "Sir,
natural affection is nothing: but affection from
principle and established duty is sometimes won-

96

derfully strong" (Life, IV, 210). On another occasion, Boswell inquired, "Is not modesty natural?"
and Johnson replied, "I cannot say, sir, as we
find no people quite in a state of nature; but I
think the more they are taught, the more modest
they are" (Life, III, 352). Elsewhere Johnson
maintained: "Pity is not natural to man. Children
are always cruel. Pity is acquired and improved
by the cultivation of reason" (Life, I, 437). On
still another occasion, Johnson spoke of one of
his acquaintances as "totally unfixed in his
principles," while Boswell excused the man--noting
that his principles had been "poisoned by a noted
infidel writer," but that he was nonetheless a
"benevolent good man." Johnson's reply is a flat
refutation of instinctive goodness:

> We can have no dependence upon that
> instinctive, that constitutional good-
> ness which is not founded upon principle.
> I grant you that such a man may be a
> very amiable member of society. I can
> conceive him placed in such a situation
> that he is not much tempted to deviate
> from what is right; and as every man
> prefers virtue, when there is not some
> strong inducement to transgress its
> precepts, I can conceive him doing
> nothing wrong. But if such a man stood
> in need of money, I should not like to
> trust him. (Life, I, 443)[8]

In a similar manner, Johnson, in the Idler no. 4,
rails against sentimentalist philosophers, who
theorize about the spontaneous good feelings of
the human heart:

> Compassion is by some reasoners,
> on whom the name of philosophers has
> been too easily conferred, resolved
> into an affection merely selfish, an
> involuntary perception of pain at the
> involuntary sight of a being like our-
> selves languishing in misery. But this
> sensation, if ever it be felt at all

97

from the brute instinct of uninstructed
nature, will only produce effects des-
ultory and transient; it will never
settle into a principle of action, or
extend relief to calamities unseen, in
generations not yet in being. (Works,
II, 13)

Johnson's attitude towards sentimentalists, or
"feelers," as he loved to call them, is well-
known. There is, for example, his portrait of
Mrs. Tim Warner, in the Idler no. 100, who daily
exercises her benevolence by pitying every misfortune that happens to every family within her
circle of notice. Her charity, however, extends
no farther than her "lamenting that so many poor
wretches should languish in the streets, and by
wondering what the great can think on that they
do so little with such large estates" (Works, II,
308 /italics mine7). Johnson's objection is that
this "good sort of woman" merely feels; she does
not act according to rational moral principle.
When Boswell once apologized to Johnson for not
feeling for others as sensibly as many say they
do, Johnson advised him not to be duped by them
any more. "You will find these very feeling
people are not very ready to do you good," he
said; "they pay you by feeling" (Life, II, 94-95).

Man's moral conduct, Johnson was keenly
aware, requires restraint over his instinctive
feelings, appetites, and passions. Reason, which
Johnson calls "the great distinction of human
nature, the faculty by which we approach to some
degree of association with celestial intelli-
gences," is the principal means of insuring such
restraint (Works, V, 95). Since reason facilitates control over man's feelings and passions,
Johnson argues in the Rambler no. 8, that the man
who "would govern his actions by the laws of virtue, must regulate his thoughts by those of reason"
(Works, III, 46). With even greater emphasis he
declares elsewhere, "He that thinks reasonably
must think morally" (Works, VII, 71).

But while Johnson viewed reason as man's
highest faculty and while he vigorously affirmed
the classical doctrine that reason must predominate over "those passions which now pruduce all
our pains and all our pleasures," he never regarded
the predominance of reason as an easy achievement,
however necessary it might be (Rambler 8, III, 43).
Nor did he believe that reason alone is sufficient
to insure moral conduct. His satiric portrait of
the stoic sage in Rasselas illustrates the all-
too-apparent limitations of even the most resolute
attempts to guide human conduct wholly by reason,
to the exclusion of feeling. Even though the
sage discourses eloquently from the "unshaken
throne of rational fortitude," he finds reason
unable to assuage the deep personal sorrow occasioned by the death of his only child (R, xviii,
85). In The Vision of Theodore, Johnson explains
allegorically the limitation of reason without
principle.⁹ Reason, which has the power only "to
advise, not to compel," is the figure charged with
conducting those who receive her laws to Religion,
"a better Guide." Unless Reason is informed by
faith and moral principle, the allegory suggests,
the dangers attributed to man's instinctive
feelings and passions will not be overcome.

In parts of Sense and Sensibility, Jane Austen
demonstrates a similar awareness of the limitations
of reason without feeling or moral principle. In
her brilliant exposition of the gradual diminution
of John Dashwood's financial assistance to his
half sisters and step-mother, for instance, Jane
Austen satirically dramatizes the danger of di-
recting conduct only by reason, to the exclusion
of moral principle and human sympathy. John
Dashwood for a time considers the benevolence of
giving Elinor, Marianne, and their mother an out-
right bequest of three-thousand pounds, but with
the calculating and dispassionate direction of
his wife, he gradually changes his mind, and di-
minishes the sum first to five-hundred, then to
one-hundred, and finally to fifty pounds "now and
then." "The assistance he /the uncle to whom the
promise of assistance was made/ thought of, I dare

say," Mrs. John Dashwood callously observes to her husband, "was only such as might be reasonably expected of you; for instance, such as looking out for a comfortable small house for them, helping them to move their things, and sending them presents of fish and game, and so forth, whenever they are in season. I'll lay my life that he meant nothing farther; indeed, it would be very strange and unreasonable if he did" (SS, 12 /Italics mine/). Reason, manipulated so selfishly, so unfeelingly, and with so little principle, leads Mrs. John Dashwood to conclude that her husband's relatives will be much more able to assist them instead!

In comparison with the opening episode, however, the major part of Sense and Sensibility does not realistically explore the complex interrelationship of feeling and reason guided by moral principle. Consider, for example, the initial descriptions of the two heroines, Elinor and Marianne:

Elinor, this eldest daughter whose advice was so effectual, possessed a strength of understanding, and coolness of judgment, which qualified her, though only nineteen, to be the counsellor of her mother, and enabled her to counteract, to the advantage of them all, that eagerness of mind in Mrs. Dashwood which must generally have led to imprudence. She had an excellent heart;--her disposition was affectionate, and her feelings were strong; but she knew how to govern them: it was a knowledge which her mother had yet to learn, and which one of her sisters had resolved never to be taught.

Marianne's abilities were, in many respects, quite equal to Elinor's. She was sensible and clever; but eager in every thing; her sorrows, her joys, could have no moderation. She was generous, amiable, interesting: she was

every thing but prudent. The resemblance
between her and her mother was strikingly
great. (SS, 6)

While Ian Watt justifiably observes that we must
abandon any attempt to view /Sense and Sensibility/
as based on an unqualified and diametrical opposition between sense and sensibility, and see
instead that Jane Austen requires us to make much
more complex discriminations between the two
terms,"[10] Jane Austen's characters never achieve
a convincing depth of personality that would
warrant complex discriminations. Elinor is supposed to have an "excellent heart," an "affectionate" disposition, and "strong" feelings that
are controlled by her "strength of understanding"
and her "coolness of judgment"; but Jane Austen
never explores the intensity of Elinor's feelings.
In a similar way, although Marianne is intended
to be "sensible and clever," we see her only in
the guise of a charming but superficial "feeler."
Marianne and Elinor, in fact, threaten invariably
to resolve into mere stereotypes, unrealistic
figures of burlesque--not psychologically complex
individuals.

     The characteristically stereotyped behavior
of Elinor and Marianne is exemplified by their
radically different responses to Elinor's suitor,
Edward Ferrars. Marianne finds him dull, and
melodramatically grieves that Edward has no "taste"
for drawing, which in her mind is defined as
"rapturous delight" (SS, 19). Elinor's response,
on the other hand, is excessively rational. "At
present, I know him so well, that I think him
really handsome; or at least, almost so," she
observes; "I do not attempt to deny . . . that I
think very highly of him--that I greatly esteem,
that I like him" (SS, 21). Indignant over such
lukewarm expression, Marianne wildly exclaims:
"Esteem him! Like him! Cold-hearted Elinor!
Oh! worse than cold-hearted! Ashamed of being
otherwise. Use those words again and I will leave
the room this moment." Elinor understandably
laughs at Marianne's excessive display of feeling,

but Elinor's rationality is equally excessive.
We may fully appreciate the rational merits of
Elinor's judgment, for it would indeed be imprudent
to risk her sentiments on Edward without further
acquaintance with him; but though she claims that
her feelings are stronger than she has declared,
she appears to have no feeling at all. Elinor is
a mere personification of rationality, not a complex personality, whose feelings are channeled
by a rational and well-principled mind. When
Elinor informs her sister that she has privately
guarded the secret of Edward's clandestine engagement to Lucy Steele, Marianne visibly wonders
how Elinor could have managed to be so rationally
self-composed during that time. "By feeling that
I was doing my duty" is Elinor's rational--and
rather mechanical--reply (SS, 262). Despite
Elinor's explanation, Marianne remains incredulous,
and so for that matter does the reader, who may
intellectually appreciate the cogency of Elinor's
argument, but who nevertheless finds it difficult
to perceive any depth of feeling in her character.
Elinor remains to the end a "type" of rationality.

Marianne, even more than Elinor, is a type,
a figure of burlesque, a caricature whose responses
to character and situation represent only the
enthusiasm and eagerness of a weak-minded "feeler."
With typical romantic excess, for example, she
complains to her mother that Elinor's reactions
are not as sensitive as hers. "Elinor, in quitting
Norland and Edward, cried not as I did," Marianne
says. "Even now her self-command is inviolable.
When is she dejected or melancholy? When does she
try to avoid society, or appear restless and dissatisfied with it?" When Willoughby mysteriously
departs for London, Marianne wildly runs from the
parlor to her room in a "violent affliction," and
does not return until dinner, when she enters the
room with eyes that are noticeably "red and
swollen" (SS, 75). She deliberately avoids her
sister's looks, and when her mother silently
presses her hand "with tender compassion,"
Marianne's "small degree of fortitude /is/ quite
overcome" (SS, 82). She bursts into tears and

leaves the room to waste away another evening in
a "violent oppression of spirits." Marianne's
whole character is so thoroughly constructed on
an "indulgence of feeling" that she unrealistically
spends entire days alone, "indulging the recollection of past enjoyment and crying over the
present," playing Willoughby's favorite songs at
the pianoforte and "alternately singing and
crying; her voice often totally suspended by her
tears." "I must feel," she says with characteristic indulgence; "I must be wretched--and they
are welcome to enjoy the consciousness of it that
can" (SS, 189-90). Even Marianne's repentance
is as excessive and as stylized as her indulgence
of feeling. Marianne is certainly right in recognizing that her irrational behavior has induced
her suffering, but her contrition is comically
unreasonable and unrealistic. Enthusiasm,
rationality, religious-moral principle are all a
part of Marianne's plan of reformation, but the
ingredients remain discrete; they never coalesce
and vitalize a psychologically complex character.

While Jane Austen fails to achieve a psychologically complex individual in either Marianne
or Elinor, she does succeed immeasurably in her
uniquely realistic portrayal of Anne Elliot in
Persuasion. Anne does not simply personify
Elinor's sense and Marianne's sensibility. Anne,
who justly claims the privilege of "loving
longest, when existence or when hope is gone,"
genuinely struggles to accommodate intense personal
feeling to the demands of reason and moral principle, and she realistically pays for that
struggle at times at the high cost of personal
suffering (P, 235). After eight years of nearly
tragic separation from Captain Wentworth because
of her voluntary submission to Lady Russell, Anne
poignantly suggests the amount of human suffering
it has cost her:

> "I have been thinking over the past,
> and trying impartially to judge of the
> right and wrong, I mean with regard to
> myself; and I must believe that I was

right, much as I suffered from it, that
I was perfectly right in being guided by
the friend whom you will love better than
you do now. To me, she was in the place
of a parent. Do not mistake me, however,
I am not saying that she did not err in
her advice. . . . But I mean, that I
was right in submitting to her, and
that if I had done otherwise, I should
have suffered more in continuing the
engagement than I did even in giving it
up, because I should have suffered in
my conscience. I have now, as far as
such a sentiment is allowable in human
nature, nothing to reproach myself with;
and if I mistake not, a strong sense of
duty is no bad part of a woman's
portion." (P, 246)

Unlike Elinor and Marianne, Anne fully actualizes
the values of sense and sensibility, and genuinely
suffers the consequences when strong personal
feeling is subordinated to reason and moral duty.

   Although Anne's share of suffering has taken
an enormous toll on her body and spirit, it has
never deterred her from accepting duty, or its
attendant hardship. In the episode with which
Persuasion begins, for example--when Sir Walter
Elliot acknowledges the family's financial diffi-
culties--Anne's suggestions for resolving them are
"all on the side of honesty against importance"
(P, 12). In glaring contrast to her vain father
and sister, Anne wishes to assume "more vigorous
measures, a more complete reformation, a quicker
release from debt, a much higher tone of indifference for every thing but justice and equity."
Anne considers it "an act of indispensable duty"
to be released from the claims of creditors as
completely and as expeditiously as possible, and
she can see "no dignity" in anything less than a
necessary form of "self-denial" and sacrifice.
Thus, while Anne dreads moving to Bath with her
family--for whom she has "no real value"--she
believes "it would be most right, and most wise,

and therefore, must involve least suffering, to
go with the others" (P, 33). Fortunately her
querulous sister Mary, who imagines she is ill
and requires Anne's attendance at Uppercross,
provides her "a different duty"; and Anne, who is
positively "glad to have any thing marked out as
a duty," agrees to stay. With remarkable "perseverance in patience, and forced cheerfulness"
Anne restores her sister to tolerable vigor (P,
39). Nursing a selfish sister, however, is the
least of Anne's duties at Uppercross. There is
"so much domestic disorder and dissension" in the
house and among the Musgrove families that Anne
voluntarily assumes the role of peacemaker. When
little Charles falls and breaks his collarbone,
Anne has "every thing to do at once," and unself-
ishly assumes to herself all the responsibilities
of the crisis (P, 56). Similarly, when Louisa
Musgrove falls from the Cobb, it is Anne who with
"strength and zeal" attends to the duties of the
moment. Anne's remarkable resilience in all her
conduct springs from what Wentworth justly calls
the "resolutions of a collected mind" and a
great "steadiness of principle" (P, 242). But
Anne's rational fidelity to principle is no conventional observance, as Elinor's often seems to
be. It is, rather, the voluntary resolution of
a genuinely sensitive individual, who has learned
through suffering and patience, reason and principle, to control and channel her feelings.

To do her complete justice, however, we must
remember that Anne's emotional life is no less
intense--though far more realistic--than Marianne's.
And Anne's intensity of feeling impresses us as
much by its conspicuous contrast with the excessive or deficient feeling of those around her as
by her own genuine rational control. Because of
her intense feeling, moreover, Anne can literally
preach rational restraint to her family and
friends, as no other Austen heroine can, and never
be charged--as Elinor Dashwood sometimes is--with
being excessively rational, self-righteous, or
unfeeling.

Anne's acquaintance with the melancholic
Captain Benwick provides one exemplary ironic--
and comic--contrast between a life of integrated
feeling, reason, and principle, and one which,
because of its excess of feeling, seems precar-
iously on the verge of disintegration. Captain
Benwick, who is shy, sedentary, and seemingly
inconsolable over the recent loss of his fiancée,
has developed a considerable taste in reading,
which enables him to discuss with Anne the rich-
ness of romantic poetry, to compare their opinions
about the quality of the poets Scott and Byron,
and to determine the relative merits of such works
as "Marmion," "The Lady of the Lake," "The Giaour,"
and "The Bride of Abydos." The general impression
conveyed by Benwick's intimate acquaintance with
"all the tenderest songs of the one poet" and
"all the impassioned descriptions of hopeless
agony of the other," by his ability to repeat
"with such tremulous feeling, the various lines
which imaged a broken heart, or a mind destroyed
by wretchedness," and by his looking "so entirely
as if he meant to be understood" is that he lib-
erally indulges his feelings and unhealthily
magnifies and flaunts them (P, 100). Anne, who
has privately suffered a longer and more intense
grief than his, keenly reacts to Benwick's display
of feeling, in this simultaneously pathetic and
comic scene, with the hope that he does not always
read only poetry and with the observation that
"it was the misfortune of poetry, to be seldom
safely enjoyed by those who enjoyed it completely"
and that "the strong feelings which alone could
estimate it truly, were the very feelings which
ought to taste it but sparingly." But Benwick is
too emotionally self-involved to recognize the
mild censure in Anne's tone of voice, and he is
rather pleased than pained with her allusion to
his sad situation. Anne therefore recommends to
him "a larger allowance of prose in his daily
study" and, in particular, "such memoirs of characters of worth and suffering, as occurred to her
at the moment as calculated to rouse and fortify
the mind by the highest precepts, and the strongest
examples of moral and religious endurances" (P,

106

101), While Benwick listens attentively and appears grateful to Anne, he only shakes his head and sighs, confessing his little faith in the power of any books--principles or reason--over strong feelings like his. With amusing irony, however, Benwick rapidly falls in love with a girl, whose only good sense seems to have been gathered by a fall on her head, tremulously recites poetry to her during her recovery, and soon marries her. By his fickleness and short-lived passion for Fanny Harville, Jane Austen dramatically demonstrates the impermanence of unguided feeling, even feeling as tremulous as Benwick's.

Anne stands convincingly and attractively not only against the emotional excess of Captain Benwick, but also against the emotional (and moral) vacuity of her sister, Mary Musgrove. When Mary's youngest child is severely injured, both Mary and her husband Charles understandably assure the elder Musgroves that, because of the child's accident, they will be unable to dine with them at the Great House that evening. The next day, however, because the child has slept restfully during the night, Charles rationalizes that he might leave the boy in Mary's hands. Besides, Anne would be at home to help Mary, he reasons. Mary, on the other hand, privately accuses her husband to Anne of being "very unfeeling" towards their son:

"I did not think Charles would have
been so unfeeling. So, here he is to
go away and enjoy himself, and because
I am the poor mother, I am not to be
allowed to stir;--and yet, I am sure, I
am more unfit than any body else to be
about the child. My being the mother
is the very reason why my feelings
should not be tried. I am not at all
equal to it. You saw how hysterical I
was yesterday." (P, 56)

Anne therefore obligingly offers to stay with the child, and Mary accepts her offer with "her eyes brightening." "Dear me, that's a very good thought, very good indeed," Mary observes; "You, who have not a mother's feelings, are a great deal the properest person" (P, 57). Mary's self-exposing remarks to Anne bristle with an almost savage irony. "I am sure I ought to go if I can," Mary selfishly rationalizes. "I shouldn't go, you may be sure," she insists, "if I did not feel quite at ease about my dear child." But without either feeling, good reason, or principle, Mary goes and leaves her child.

We can recognize and appreciate the intensity of Anne's properly directed feelings, then, partly by conspicuous contrast with the emotional deficiency or excess of other characters. But we can appreciate Anne's intensity of feeling most of all (and almost paradoxically) by the degree of rational restraint she exercises in her encounters with Captain Wentworth. Consider, for example, Wentworth's return and brief visit to Uppercross Cottage, where Anne has been sojourning. Wentworth's visit is so brief that Jane Austen disposes of it in less than a paragraph:

Mary, very much gratified by this attention /Wentworth's visit7, was delighted to receive him; while a thousand feelings rushed on Anne, of which this was the most consoling, that it would soon be over. And it was soon over. In two minutes after Charles's preparation, the others appeared; they were in the drawing-room. Her eye half met Captain Wentworth's; a bow, a curtsey passed; she heard his voice--talked to Mary, said all that was right; said something to the Miss Musgroves, enough to mark an easy footing: the room seemed full--full of persons and voices--but a few minutes ended it. Charles shewed himself at the window, all was ready, their visitor bowed and was gone; the Miss Musgroves were gone too, suddenly resolving to walk to the

end of the village with the sportsmen:
the room was cleared, and Anne might
finish her breakfast as she could.
(P, 59-60)

It is not difficult to believe that Anne and
Wentworth once enjoyed a period of "exquisite
felicity" together, when they had fallen "rapidly
and deeply in love," for Anne, even in this brief
accidental encounter with Wentworth, is obviously
still deeply moved by him. In her meeting with
Wentworth after eight long years of separation,
"a thousand feelings rushed on Anne." The scene
appears to be written with a narrator's objectivity,
yet the rapid cadence of such short, almost breath-
less, phrases--"her eye half met Captain
Wentworth's; a bow, a curtsey passed; she heard
his voice"--dramatically suggests the "agitation"
that stirs Anne's heart and mind. Even after
eight years, Wentworth can cause in her a nervous
excitement. Their restrained encounter lasts
only a few minutes, but at the end of it, Anne is
left alone--with more convincing inner tremulous-
ness than Marianne or Captain Benwick ever could
muster--"to finish her breakfast as she could"
(P, 60).

For sheer intense feeling Persuasion is not
easily surpassed. Jane Austen has all the materials for creating a romantic love story, but she
deliberately restrains her heroine in order to
create a greater, and more believable emotional
intensity. Early in the novel, Jane Austen uses
the conventional language of romance: Anne and
Wentworth had fallen "rapidly and deeply in love"
and had enjoyed a period of "exquisite felicity."
But throughout the period of Anne's renewed encounters with Wentworth, the author undercuts
the overt display of feeling with Anne's subjective wondering, suffering, and restraint. When
Wentworth places Anne in Admiral Croft's carriage
after the long and tiring walk to Winthrop, for
example, Anne is left to question in painful silence the certainty of Wentworth's love for her:

Yes,--he had done it. She was in
the carriage, and felt that he had placed
her there, that his will and his hands
had done it, that she owed it to his
perception of her fatigue, and his resolution to give her rest; . . . She understood him. He could not forgive her,--
but he could not be unfeeling. Though
condemning her for the past, and considering it with high and unjust
resentment, though perfectly careless
of her, and though becoming attached to
another, still he could not see her
suffer, without the desire of giving
her relief. It was a proof of his own
warm and amiable heart, which she could
not contemplate without emotions so
compounded of pleasure, and pain, that
she knew not which prevailed. (P, 91)

In this encounter Anne reveals herself as a psychologically credible woman whose emotions are
understandably "compounded of pleasure and pain"--
pleasure, in recognizing the nature of Wentworth's
feelings, and pain, in remembering her termination
of their engagement. Indeed, Anne endures the
pain and responsibility of separation from
Wentworth throughout most of Persuasion--as when
even in their accidental late encounter in
Molland's shop, Anne experiences "agitation, pain,
pleasure, a something between delight and misery"
(P, 175). Anne's genuine love for Wentworth and
her growing recognition of his love for her, in
fact, are invariably checked by Anne's strong
sense of pain and responsibility for having once
deferred to the authority of Lady Russell. Thus,
when Anne finally discovers the certainty of
Wentworth's love, Jane Austen justifiably returns
to the conventional language of romance, por-
traying Anne's "musings of high-wrought love and
eternal constancy" which are "almost enough to
spread purification and perfume all the way" along
the streets of Bath--because by her fidelity to
principle and by her rational restraint, even
under suffering, Anne has truly earned this ro-

mantic ecstasy. By realistically sustaining
Anne's agitation during her encounters with
Wentworth, by emphasizing the natural rhythm and
tension of Anne's pleasure and pain, and by in-
tegrating in one character the otherwise discrete
ingredients of reason, principle, and feeling,
Jane Austen creates a genuinely convincing and
attractive heroine in a novel of restrained
emotional intensity.

In Persuasion, in other words, Jane Austen
explores the same Johnsonian theme she had earlier
attempted unsuccessfully in Sense and Sensibility--
the subordination of feeling to reason and moral
principle. But while in the first novel her
characters Elinor and Marianne are mere personi-
fications of reason and feeling, who clearly
derive from an eighteenth-century moral schema-
tization, her psychologically realistic portrait
of Anne Elliot, in whom reason and moral principle
are vitalized by intense personal feeling, signals
a unique success in the representation of character
with profound dramatic effect. Far from indicating
a departure from her Johnsonian moral ethos,
Persuasion rather signifies how thoroughly Jane
Austen had absorbed it in her artistically mature
work.

NOTES

[1]Marvin Mudrick, _Jane Austen: Irony as Defense and Discovery_ (1952; rpt. Berkeley: University of California Press, 1968), p. 90.

[2]A. Walton Litz, _Jane Austen: A Study of Her Artistic Development_ (New York: Oxford University Press, 1965), p. 154.

[3]Howard S. Babb, _Jane Austen's Novels: The Fabric of Dialogue_ (Columbus, Ohio: Ohio State University Press, 1962), p. 203.

[4]Litz, p. 82. The author succinctly explains the nature of these artistic conventions: "The titles _Sense and Sensibility_ and _Pride and Prejudice_ derive from a standard thematic pattern set by late eighteenth-century moralistic fiction, in which opposed qualities of mind are dramatized through opposed personalities, usually sisters or close friends of radically different temperaments. Of course Jane Austen sought to modify this anti-thetical structure in creating _Sense and Sensibility_, and she transformed it almost beyond recognition in the final version of _Pride and Prejudice_, where it would be difficult to associate the hero with one particular quality and the heroine with its opposite. But the rigid anti-thetical form was her starting point in both novels, and in _Sense and Sensibility_ she never escaped from it; we are still justified in saying that Marianne represents Sensibility while Elinor stands for Sense" (pp. 73-74).

[5]Quoted in William E. Alderman, "Shaftesbury and the Doctrine of Moral Sense in the Eighteenth Century," _PMLA_, 46 (1931), 1087.

[6]Alderman, p. 1088.

[7]Sir John Hawkins, _The Life of Samuel Johnson, LL.D._, ed. Bertram H. Davis (New York: Macmillan, 1961), p. 215.

[8]Notice the resemblance of Johnson's observation with a familiar passage in Emma, in which
Mr. Knightley explains his disapproval of Frank
Churchill: "There is one thing, Emma, which a
man can always do, if he chuses, and that is, his
duty; not by manoeuvring and finessing, but by
vigour and resolution. It is Frank Churchill's
duty to pay this attention to his father. . . .
Your amiable young man is a very weak young man,
if this be the first occasion of his carrying
through a resolution to do right against the will
of others. It ought to have been an habit with
him by this time, of following his duty, instead
of consulting expediency. I can allow for the
fears of the child, but not of the man. As he
became rational, he ought to have roused himself
and shaken off all that was unworthy in their
/his adopted family's/ authority. He ought to
have opposed the first attempt on their side to
make him slight his father. Had he begun as he
ought, there would have been no difficulty
now. . . . No, Emma, your amiable young man can
be amiable only in French, not in English. He
may be very 'aimable,' have very good manners,
and be very agreeable; but he can have no English
delicacy towards the feelings of other people:
nothing really amiable about him" (E, 146-49).

[9]The Works of Samuel Johnson, LL.D. (1787;
rpt. Oxford: Oxford University Press, 1825), IX,
162-75.

[10]Ian Watt, "On Sense and Sensibility,"
Introduction to Sense and Sensibility (1961), rpt.
in Ian Watt, ed., Jane Austen: A Collection of
Critical Essays (Englewood Cliffs, N.J.:
Prentice-Hall, 1963), pp. 46-47.

EPILOGUE

Recognizing her Johnsonian moral heritage can--as we have seen--resolve many of the questions which a twentieth-century critical sensibility raises about Jane Austen's novels. Traditional concepts like self-deception and self-knowledge, the misleading imagination and reliable common sense, rational self-control, discipline and sacrifice--explored extensively by her favorite prose moralist Dr. Samuel Johnson-- invariably increase our capacity to appreciate a dimension of her fiction that derives from an orthodox, eighteenth-century English Christianity.

Morality, in other words, is an inseparable part of Jane Austen's artistic achievement. By identifying the Johnsonian moral norms which inform her novels and by demonstrating the manner and the extent to which they are assimilated, in the illustration of character, the determination of incident, and the exploration of theme, the preceding chapters question the fairness of criticism which denies the unity of her moral and her artistic impulse. F. R. Leavis vigorously reminds us of this unity when he says of one of her greatest novels that "the formal perfection of Emma . . . can be appreciated only in terms of the moral preoccupations that characterize the novelist's peculiar interest in life."[1] What Leavis says of Emma may be said, too, of the other major novels--with the singular exception of Sense and Sensibility. And there the problem is not the variance of Jane Austen's artistic and moral impulse, but the inability to explore fully in fictional characters the complexities which her Johnsonian moral heritage doubtless made available to her.

That it is a Johnsonian heritage with which Jane Austen's best work is fully endowed should remind us, moreover, of the appreciable differences between their world and ours, and between their eighteenth-century conception of human nature, with its circumscribed potentialities

and clearly defined moral responsibilities, and
our post-Darwinian, post-Freudian perceptions of
man in his ethical relativity and seemingly illim-
itable possibilities. Calling attention to these
ever increasing differences, in his lecture entitled De Descriptione Temporum, C. S. Lewis
cogently observed:

> The greatest of all divisions in the
> history of the West is that which
> divides the present from, say, the age
> of Jane Austen and Scott. The dating
> of such things must of course be rather
> hazy and indefinite. No one could point
> to a year or a decade in which the change
> indisputably began, and it has probably
> not yet reached its peak. But somewhere
> between us and the Waverly Novels, some-
> where between us and Persuasion, the
> chasm runs.[2]

It is not insignificant that Lewis chose Persuasion
to represent the vague, indefinable boundary
between that age and ours, for even in her last
completed novel Jane Austen maintained her
allegiance to a traditional moral ethos which,
though discernably different from ours, may yet
speak to us across these two hundred years with
impressive clarity, conviction, and authority.

NOTES

[1]F. R. Leavis, The Great Tradition: George Eliot, Henry James, Joseph Conrad (1948; rpt. New York: George W. Stewart, n. d.), p. 8.

[2]C. S. Lewis, They Asked for a Paper: Papers and Addresses (London: Geoffrey Bles, 1962), p. 17.

INDEX

Adventurer, The, 10,
  11, 38, 50
Alderman, William E.,
  112n
Alkon, Paul Kent, 91n
attention, 44-50
Austen, Cassandra, 5
Austen, George, 9
Austen, Henry, 5, 9
Austen, James, 9
Austen-Leigh, James
  Edward, 5, 9, 12n,
  91n

Babb, Howard, 93, 112n
Berkeley, Bishop
  George, 17
Blair, Dr. Hugh, 10
Blake, William, 34n
Book of Common Prayer,
  38
Boswell, James, 3, 5,
  6, 7, 11, 17, 96, 97
Bradbrook, Frank, 4,
  12n
Bradley, A. C., 2-3,
  12n

Chapman, R. W. 9, 12n,
  34n, 62n
Characteristics of Men,
  Manners, Opinions,
  Times, 95
Christianity, 2, 8,
  38, 66, 115
Coleridge, Samuel
  Taylor, 34n
common sense, 2, 4, 16,
  27, 28, 29, 33, 38,
  115
Conduct of the Under-
  standing, 50, 62n

Cooper, Edward, 9
Cowper, William, 5, 6,
  43
Crabbe, George, 5, 7,
  49

Dictionary of the
  English Language, A,
  11, 18, 68, 72, 75
discipline, 37, 38, 55,
  57, 58, 59, 115
Duckworth, Alistair M.,
  15, 34n
Duffy, Joseph, 37n, 61n
duty, 2, 56, 104

Emma, 10, 11, 21, 60,
  65-92, 115
Essay Concerning Human
  Understanding, An,
  16, 17, 44, 61n

Fancy, 17-35
Farrer, Reginald, 37,
  61n
Fielding, Henry, 7, 96
Fowler, Thomas, 63n
Fraser, Alexander
  Campbell, 61n

Garrod, H. W., 65, 91n
Gothic, 15, 24, 25, 27

Habit, 50-55, 57, 59
Hagstrum, Jean, 34n
Hardship, 37, 38, 39,
  53-59, 103-106
Havens, Raymond D., 34n
Hawkins, Sir John, 96,
  112n
Hutcheson, Francis, 95

Idler, The, 4, 7, 10,
  11, 38, 44, 49, 50,
  68, 79, 81, 83, 97,
  98
Imagination, 15-35

Journal of a Tour to
  the Hebrides, 5
Journey to the Western
  Islands of Scotland,
  A, 5

Kaye-Smith, Sheila, 91n
Krutch, Joseph Wood,
  34n

Lascelles, Mary, 3-4,
  12n
Leavis, F. R., 115,
  117n
Lerner, Laurence, 9,
  12n
Lewis, C. S., 4, 12n,
  116, 117n
Life of Samuel Johnson,
  The, 7, 10, 11, 17,
  51, 97, 98
Litz, A. Walton, 5, 15,
  34n, 37n, 61n, 93-94,
  112n
Lives of the English
  Poets, The, 74-75
Locke, John, 16-17, 18,
  23, 33, 34n, 35n, 44,
  50, 61n

MacLean, Kenneth, 35n
Mansfield Park, 2, 6,
  10, 11, 21, 33, 37-
  63, 67, 94, 95
McIntosh, Carey, 12n
McKillop, Alan D., 35n
Memory, 40-50, 59
Moler, Kenneth L., 35n,
  91n

Monk, The, 8
Mudrick, Marvin, 1, 2,
  12n, 37n, 61n, 65,
  91n, 93, 112n
Mysteries of Udolpho,
  The, 31-32

Northanger Abbey, 6,
  8, 10, 11, 15-35

Persuasion, 3, 6, 10,
  11, 21, 89, 90, 93-
  113, 116
pride, 2, 38, 66, 67-
  74, 83-84, 89
Pride and Prejudice, 3,
  10, 11, 20, 60, 65-
  92

Radcliffe, Mrs. Ann,
  15, 29, 32
Rambler, The, 4, 8, 9,
  10, 11, 16, 19, 28,
  30, 31, 32, 33, 38,
  39, 40-41, 43, 44,
  48, 50, 55, 56, 67,
  68, 74, 75, 77, 79,
  80, 81, 82, 83, 87,
  88, 98, 99
Rasselas, 7, 8, 10, 11,
  16, 17, 19, 20, 54-
  55, 96, 99
reason, 4, 15, 16, 20,
  23, 48, 93-113
reflection, 81-86, 89
Richardson, Samuel, 7
Roderick Random, 8

sacrifice, 2, 37, 38,
  59, 104, 115
Schorer, Mark, 65, 66,
  91n
Scott, Walter, 106, 116
self-knowledge, 2, 38,
  60, 65-92, 115

Sense and Sensibility,
3, 11, 20, 93-113, 115
Shaftesbury, Lord, 95,
96, 112n
Sherlock, Bishop, 9,
10
Sir Charles Grandison,
7
Spectator, The, 38
Staunton, George, 17
Stern, G. B., 65, 91n

Tatler, The, 38
Tom Jones, 7, 8
Trilling, Lionel, 15,
62n

Vanity of Human Wishes,
The, 68
Vision of Theodore,
The, 99
Voitle, Robert, 12n,
61n

Watt, Ian, 7, 12n, 35n,
91n, 101, 113n
Watts, Isaac, 18
Wilson, Edmund, 65,
91n
Wordsworth, William,
34n
Wright, Andrew, 15, 34n